Tyneside Tales

Tyneside Tales

ISBN 0-9549363-4-5

Published and distributed by
ENDpapers Ltd
Collage Corner, 2 Norman Court
YORK, YO1 7HU
www.endpapers.co.uk

First published November 2005
Printed by Fratelli Spada, Italy

Credits

Text
Editor:	Rachel Hazelwood
Proofreaders:	Julia Key and Ruth Wilson
Readers:	Florence Millett
	Peter Johnson

Images
ENDpapers/photography:	Nick Mowbray
Cover design:	Ian Forster

Production
Design and typesetting:	gavin ward design associates
Production Manager:	Sally Mowbray
Project co-ordinator:	Florence Millett

Competition Judges
Jill Morris	BORDERS Bookshop, Silver Link, Tyneside
Pauline Hughes	Leader of the Northumbria MA in Creative Writing
Celia Bryce	Writer and singer
Ruth Henderson	Author
Kate Fox	Poet and newsreader Galaxy 105/6

Contents

Introduction

Tyneside was a long shot for END*papers*. Although it is relatively near to York, there was no knowledge of anyone on the ground. There were no natural networks. As each volume in the **TALES series** begins with one local contact, shed loads of leaflets, and the launch of a writing competition, things did not look easy at the outset.

As with each of the 2005 volumes in the **TALES series**, BORDERS stores had a significant role to play and acted as the first local point of call. The staff at Silver Link provided an initial impetus and enthusiasm for **TYNESIDE TALES**, disseminating information, acting as a clearing house for enquiries, and generally making it known, as widely as possible, that here was a chance for local writers to apply their skills and be published.

Not being in the city centre meant having to work harder to get notice for the competition, calling in favours from local media, communicating with writers' groups and creative writing courses and generally putting it about that submitting a story for **TYNESIDE TALES** was something worth considering.

The **TALES series** throughout the UK is providing a platform to progress local writers' opportunities. At the same time it has given writers a vehicle through which to represent their areas in all their variety. In the case of Tyneside it has been a chance to celebrate a past which has been at times both glorious yet painful, at times a past only to be survived.

The stories in this volume also provide a lead-in to a future. Tyneside is now beginning to shape itself: developments along the waterfront, a growth and stabilising of the local economy and a continual development as a cultural centre for both the north east of England and for Europeans more widely are all contributing factors.

Of the volumes of **TALES** produced in 2005, given the paucity of connection between Tyneside and END*papers*, the **TYNESIDE TALES** have been the most surprising. In effect, END*papers* flew blind in selecting Tyneside. BORDERS in Newcastle also took a risk in trying to promote something like this at arm's length from the mainstream of city life.

Yet the instinctive view was proven correct. It was simply this. Here was a region in the UK, with a melodic dialect and a history of cultural diversity within a contained sense of identity. Somehow it was believed that this would yield a rich source of short story writing.

It seems now that this view was right.

Maggi Jackson
END*papers*

Jill Morris
BORDERS, Silver Link, Newcastle

The Geordie Indieboy's Tale

James Darton

In trouble to be troubled

Is to have your trouble doubled

Daniel Defoe

I'm in Jesmond and it's a Tuesday night but maybe it's a Monday cos I'm still relatively straight and there's no wine bottle to my lips or eyeliner on my eyes and I'm at Jackson's party, milling around as the old indieboy is wont to do, in that oh-so-fey, finger-clicking, fuck-strutting way.

Predictably, the Libertines are playing in the background – y' know, 'An ending fitting for a start…' – and I walk into the front room and there's dancing and pulling and deepdeepdeep conversation and fighting and a really big telly filling the room and a very beautiful person with skinskinskin-tight Levi's approaches me, kisses me, and walks off and whether they're male or female I could not say.

I fall gracefully back on to a green sofa and a guy who is either Ed Daniels or Toby Kirkland slinks along to next to me and I turn away to admire the CD rack or something and I turn back and he's still there staring at me, expectantly like.

"Hi, Ed," I say.

He says, "Silly, it's Toby. Where've you been recently?"

And I look at him or past him or through him as he pulls a wrap of coke from his pocket, fingers it delicately and returns it to his pocket and I open my mouth to reply but can't because the simple fact is that I've not been here or there or anywhere.

It's later and I'm dancing I think (hands in pockets, staring at the floor, occasionally stamping my wooden heeled slip-ons or yelping along). My good friend Peter is facing me and we dance close so that our breath is strong and our eyeliner almost touching, yet all the while keeping our cheekbones and jaw lines under the light, facing the two girls with the razor-sharp fringes and drainpipe jeans giggling in the corner. Over Peter's shoulder I'm vaguely aware of a young girl – fourteen? – walking out of Jackson's bedroom rubbing her wrists and her eyes and there's shouting and laughter behind her and she gets her jacket and my mouth is dry again and three boys come out of the room high-fiving and being proper jocks but no one says anything and I carry on dancing and flirting and she leaves forever.

Later, lying on a bed, forcing the words:
   "I'm sorry Sophie."
   "What for?" she murmurs, stoned.
   I tell her that I'm not sure, and I'm crying as I buckle up my belt and I'm not really crying, just tears falling. For a moment I ponder the difference. As I exit the room I notice a crib in the corner, just as two guys, lost in the excesses of sex and substances, crash through the door and on to the bed next to Sophie, who may or may not be my girlfriend.

I'm in the kitchen looking for either bread or tequila and Peter falls into me, hugging me, puppy dog smile.
   He asks me what I'm doing and I tell him I'm hungry and he asks if I have any pills and I tell him no and he shakes his head and asks me if I want to dance and I tell him no and he tells me I've changed and he walks away shaking his head and I look in a cupboard and find some Warburton's Granary.
   I'm chewchewchewing away when one of the pretty fringes nudges me with her foot and says:
   "Please may you come to the shop with me as my glass is empty and I have forgotten my fake ID?"
   She's making circles on the floor with her toe and her bottom lip is all sort of *plump* looking. I pretend not to notice and I'm pretty sure I don't care anyway, as I suck in my cheeks and nod to her request.
   The girl smiles chirpily, her tongue caught impishly between her teeth, and skips off ahead of me towards the huge

Georgian door. I grab my size ten leather jacket and follow her. A pretty blond boy who could be fifteen or twenty-five or a girl grabs my hand as we leave and begs me to "just at least acknowledge my existence, please?"

I smile uncertainly and kiss him on the cheek and the girl I'm with kisses me on the mouth hard and then the boy's scratching at his wrists and his big blue eyes follow the girl and me as we leave the house, skip down the path and run down the bare and glamorous street, direction of the city.

And we're laughing and running and holding hands and this girl is holding my hand and it's great and I'm crying again and I don't know why and her ra-ra skirt is twirling and my neckerchief is strangling me and I'm coughing and laughing and crying and I don't know why.

Suddenly, the girl veers right and we're through a gap in the railings and we're in the park and we're spinning round and round and again she kisses me and she reaches to her handbag, sweating and frantic. And then I see the track marks on her arms.

It's autumn I think and we're standing under a great big oak tree, wider than you and me put together. There are gnarly, ugly bits of bark and then the smoothest most chestnut-coloured bits on its magnificent trunk and though there's no wind these majestically crisp leaves fall and fall and fall. One falls at my feet and I try really hard to see the wonder of nature, the beauty of the seasons and the seeds, the power of a purepurepure world. All I see is maybe soil and the rushing dirty brown fizz of the girl's eyes rolling back in her head.

I tell the girl that, "Y'know, I'm not really, y'know, *cool* with this," and maybe she replies but probably she doesn't.

So I'm walking back to the party all sort of...*dejectedly* isn't the right word but it's the only one in my head.

Yeah so I'm walking back to the party and I'm passing the couples kissing and the dealers dealing and the druggies – *fucking druggies* – dying, and I'm wondering why and if I'm here – you know, *really* here – and I can't make my mind up so I fall up the stairs and into the front room and downdowndown onto the couch.

Heavily drunk now, twirling to the Libertines, mumbling under my breath: *"An ending fitting for a start, You twisted and tore our love apart…"*

And then Sophie is standing in the doorway and she looks at me and I look at her and my mouth is dry, still twirling, still tears and she walks towards me and straight past me and I might shout and I might follow her with my eyes and she's so beautiful and she's so thin and she's so beautiful and it strikes me as not odd how much she looks like a corpse.

It's about four-thirty in the morning now, the party is over and everyone is being ushered out into the streets. Mum rings me and asks if I'll be home soon.

"Why?" I ask.

Because she's worried about me.

I tell her, "shutupshutupshutupshutupshutupshutup" and I'm screaming, whispering, frantic and she takes this for maybe five minutes before choking back a sob and hanging up.

Redundant isn't the right word but it's the only one in my head.

Sitting on the kerb, head in my hands, jacket around my arse. Someone tells me there's "a great after-party round mine dude" and I start crying softly to myself, possibly because of the Americanism, possibly because of all the rich-kids milling around in their thrift-store clothing blissfully unaware of the pale thin girl I'm cradling in my arms. Maybe it's just because of the coke. Maybe it's just because the entire universe is spiralling away above the lamp-posts and perfectly pruned hedges blissfully unaware of my problems and Sophie's problems and your problems. I cry some more and start rubbing my hands a bit more and scare myself a bit more by noticing that this girl, well this girl…I mean it's Sophie – but this girl Sophie, well her lips are becoming increasingly blue.

You know, the only thing that *is* certain, the only thing that I definitely know, above all the piss and the shit and the lies, is that, though none of it matters, it all matters: the drugs and the sex and the music and the clothes and the interior design and the gourmet burgers. We drift along because we have nothing else to do and we're rich and young and good-looking and I hate it.

I rub my hands a bit more and the dingy blood on them slowly comes into focus. People mill past some laughing some singing some screaming. My hands are cold and I smile because they remind me of an art class from primary school where I painted the table instead of the canvas. For the first time it feels silly that I'm not sure what I feel like right now – I'm not crying but tears are falling, I'm not sad but I'm not happy. I am exactly as I always am, aren't I?

I stand up and in front of me is Sophie's head, now resting delicately on the kerb, and I know that despite her perfect skin and perfect body and perfect maths score, her eyes are closed and her lips blue and her hair matted with blood. It strikes me as odd that I know exactly what's expected or required of me – I mean, I'll scream now for help and someone'll come and take her away and sort her out and comb her hair and me, I'll go see Peter, make things right again, escape this synthetic 'scene', console Sophie's parents and tell them how loved and valued she was and mourn her and weep for her so much that the sky caves in on itself.

But then I look behind me. It's a beautiful morning and I could sososo easily turn around and escape into the light or into a job or into another party and perhaps have a real realisation that, y'know, I've got to change or perhaps just have a real realisation that, *y'know*, things will never change. I look down at the kerb and somewhere above me a bird breaks the silence of early-morning indecision. I rub my eyes and set about doing what, for the first time in as long as I can remember, I know I have to.

Escape isn't the right word but it's the only one in my head.

A Brother's Tale

Matt Charnock

We all do things like this; we have a stone that we keep in our pocket which is a guarantee of life's continuity, and it has to do with hoping that things will all work out, that life will be okay.

Antony Gormley

Mobile phones amaze me, how they can put you in contact with anyone at any time. Like now. I am sitting in the Pitcher & Piano on Newcastle's Quayside and my sister, who is sitting opposite, is yapping away to someone at work about something at work which was causing many problems at work, though with all the talk there doesn't seem to be any actual work going on. This, however, is not my main gripe. It amazes me how mobile phones can put you in contact with anyone at any time – save the people you are actually with. Say there are four of you in a car and one in the back is on their phone; the other three are silent! Why? So as not to interrupt the person who is being rude in the first place.

My sister eventually finishes the conversation and then turns to me and repeats, word for word, the conversation I have just heard! She informs me that Michelle has done this, which means James can't do the other, and that I shouldn't even get her started on Toni from accounts. The fact that I don't even know who Toni from accounts *is* remains irrelevant as the barrage of shop talk comes relentlessly at me. Naturally, I nod and tut in the right places – I even let out a little giggle at one point to agree – and as she continues her chat I continue to feign interest. Eventually, the noise stops and she says something which sounds much more appealing. She offers me a pint of Stella. I agree to partake wholeheartedly and she leaves.

I sit back in my leather sofa like some Tyneside kingpin and eye up some of the talent that Newcastle has to offer, and I can see Geordies are quite clearly gifted. Geordies have a look that no other people have, a wild frenzy in the eye which often reveals itself in a cheeky wink or a glint from the light bouncing off the chrome-plated drinks taps. They seem full of desire, passion and mischief – they want to conquer, which probably all harks back to when the Vikings invaded. You can tell that there is Nordic blood in them. My gaze pans round and out of the huge glass walls that surround the Pitcher & Piano, revealing the River Tyne. On the Gateshead side, the Baltic stands uninterestingly near the Sage. A giant glass peanut of a building, demanding attention, flirting with its curvaceous edges, a nod to the rippling edges of the river below. All the buildings seem to shout out "Come and have a go if you think you're hard enough, pet!" in an unyielding Geordie accent – one that would usually slip from the mouth of a character from some sitcom we don't quite believe. "If you're lucky it will wink," says my sister, through the cacophony of Geordie-voiced buildings.

"What?" I ask, while receiving a deliciously frosted glass of Stella.

"The bridge," she continues, gesturing towards what I, at first glance, take to be a large buckled bicycle wheel. "It tips – it's the Millennium Eye so when it tips to let large ships through it looks like it's winking."

"Bollocks," I scoff.

"Seriously!" insists my sister, hurt at the accusation that her information on the bridge is less than genuine.

"Wow!" is the one word I can muster to describe it as she slumps into the overly large sofa opposite. We restart our conversation in the usual way – I ask her about work, she repeats the conversation I've heard twice already, explaining how without her the place would crumble – Yada yada… Next she asks me about my work. My answer starts with a sharp intake of breath and some sort of 'don't get me started on my job' noise, before I tell her that basically everything is fine and that I love a job that in reality I am really rather bored with. This is how every one of our conversations starts, and who am I to mess with tradition? She sips supportively on her white wine spritzer, each sip giving her the energy to nod and appear to be listening to what I am saying. Eventually, as we both pretend to listen to each other, the conversation moves inevitably on to my love life (or lack thereof). She informs me that she has a few single friends who she would be more than happy to set me up with, and I smile politely, completing that particular part of the routine.

Our drinks are drunk, which I take as a signal to go to the bar, allowing us a pit stop from the mundane and offering an opportunity to think of something else to talk about. Naturally, these rituals have led me to question the necessity to talk at all. The place is filling up a little and standing on either side of me are couples who, having just finished their work, are standing talking about work.

Bruce Springsteen once sang: "It struck me kind of funny – seemed kind of funny sir to me – how at the end of every hard earned day people find some reason to believe".

I look over to my sister who has started on the phone again. I order my drinks, pay and take them back to the table. As my sister is still talking on the phone, I politely sit down in silence, quietly placing her drink in front of her and raising my eyebrows as if to say "Here you go", while hinting at the fact that I am unhappy with her constant phone use.

"Thanks," she mouths back, obviously not wanting the person on the phone to think that she's thanking them for something, and then continues talking to someone who I assume to be her boyfriend. I tune out and continue people-watching. A pair of the nicest legs walks by, leading up to a very fine arse. Hands lean in and start to take the glasses from the table.

"Is this finished?" asks a voice I believe is reserved just for me.

"Err…yeah…I think. The glasn gribsd uonmby jocj," I answer intelligently. I have lost all ability to communicate and can't think like a monkey, let alone like a man, but I can't leave it on that note and so I start to hand over glasses. I'm making a ham-fisted attempt to flirt with empty beer glasses. I am flirting with glasses. Not surprisingly, I am left alone.

"Well, you will be pleased to know my boyfriend is finally on his way," says my sister, her voice slapping me back into reality, slapping my gaze away from a certain arse as it bends over a table for a glass. I hope that I may get a glance, a look, a kiss, a number, a wink, but not even the bridge winks.

"Why is he coming here? I thought that you were meeting him later?" I gasp, as all sweat evacuates from my body by the nearest pore; most of it exits via my palms and I nearly lose the grip of my pint – nearly but not quite.

"What's the matter? I thought you liked him?"

"I do, he's great, but I just wasn't expecting him, I thought it was just us two, I might have worn… Why is he coming here?" I gasp, I gag, I gargle.

"How many times?" exclaims my sister. "We are having our dance class in here tonight." A frightening smile creeps across her face.

"Dance class?" I stammer, knowing full well what she means: I'm to dance as well.

"Yes!" she smiles almost laughing. "We thought you might like it – you might meet someone." My heart didn't so much sink as stop, panic, hide behind my liver and shit itself. This is it. This is how I am going to die, I think. I am not a dancer, and teaching me to dance would be like teaching sign language to a snake. I have no rhythm and two left feet, which, when I dance, are wearing shoes that don't fit. To compensate for my lack of talent, I frantically wave my arms like I'm conducting the orchestra of the Society For The Musically Challenged. It is this that has led me down the path of the confirmed non-dancer. Now I sit back with a beverage and mock those who do dance – that is what those who don't dance do. It's a similar phenomenon to the overweight, drunk football fan telling Wayne Rooney where he is going wrong. I want out but I know that my sister won't just let me watch. Ironically, I will for my phone to ring, for a flash flood, my last hope being that my sister's boyfriend will by some miracle have dug three tunnels named Tom, Dick and Harry. My sister's boyfriend proves to be no help in my escape and turns up promptly and looking good. Really good. He brings over our drinks.

"Alreet?" comes his thick Geordie accent, dripping with self-assurance. His grin is so wide it couldn't hide the truth. He was the mastermind behind the getting me dancing plan, otherwise known as Operation Embarrass.

"Yes – great," I spit through gritted teeth.

"You'll be fine man, once the danca' gets hea' you'll have a reet laugh."

"Excellent," I reply, hoping some sniper on top of the Sage has me firmly in his sight. A noise jolts out of the blue; my heart peers from round the back of my liver in anticipation of being saved. My sister's phone is ringing – is this my ticket out of this hell? No. Some crisis which Michelle, James and Toni from accounts can't fix demands that my sister return to work before the building collapses, leaving me alone with my sister's boyfriend. In times of great stress people try different techniques in order to help them through it. It is interesting how people cope with stressful situations. Some meditate, some pray to their god, others seek help from a dead relative, some stroke their wedding band. Somehow we find that thing within us, that moment of strength that urges us to just get on with it. Me, I drink. I down my pint of Stella.

As we get onto the dance floor we take our positions. Naturally, I am the girl in the partnership. I feel eyes looking at me and my sister's boyfriend, the only all-male couple. My hand ventures forth and takes hold of his waist. His hand slides round to the small of my back. He laughs; I sweat.

He pulls me closer; I feign resistance.

His other hand takes hold of my hand.

The click and strike of a Cuban heel on a highly polished floor buries the sound of my pounding heart.

I hold him tighter.

"Fea' can be a remarkable stimulus," crows my sister's boyfriend.

"Really?" I offer. "Who said that? Nietzsche? Socrates?" I try desperately to lose myself in idle chitchat.

"Na man, Getafix the Druid from Asterix," he sniggers. Despair takes over my body as I look into my partner's eyes. My eyes flick from his lips to his eyes, to his lips, to his ear, to his cheek, his hairline, back to his lips. He seems to squeeze me tighter – I want to kiss him, to taste him, devour him like he has devoured me. The music starts, some Latin, up-tempo nonsense that could never appeal to the ear of the petrified.

On the quayside I see people begin to stop; the laid-back, European cultural feel now means that these people, these laid-back, cultured Europeans, with nothing better to do, are standing by all the windows and watching my hell. As I stand there in the arms of a man in the Pitcher & Piano on Newcastle's quayside I take back everything I have thought about Newcastle's glass being an unashamed expression of its new self. Cursing the damned architects, I realise all too well that the problem with the glass is that people can see me dancing with my sister's boyfriend, but, moreover, can see inside me.

As this thought balloons in my brain, under the watch of a rusty angel, a certain bridge winks at me and I don't want the dance to end.

The Tale of Micka's Christmas

Frances Kay

keep your feet still, Geordie hinny,

lets be happy through the neet

For we may not be so happy through the day;

So give us that bit of comfort,

keep your feet still, Geordie lad,

And divvent drive me bonny dreams away.

George Ridley

17

At the shops in Walker Street it is like being a ghost and treading in the streets of heaven. There is white everywhere, pretend snow and starry lights and glitter stuff stuck on the windows, and all this white makes you forget to see the dirty bits of the street.

I watch the window with Snow White and the Seven Dwarfs moving. It is only machines but it looks more like real if you shut your eyes a bit. Snow White looks dead real. Her smile is all soft like Mam when she drinks whisky and we have the fire lit and she sits by it with the red of the flames shining over her. Snow White with a blue dress and curls spun out from her face, stiff like black candy floss. And she keeps always waving to the dwarfs, and they shove presents in her arms, all done up smart in boxes with paper and silver stars and bows. My friend Shane says there is nothing inside the boxes, but that is a lie. We saw the little kids in Galloways with their mams in a line to see Santa. Some crying. Scared of Santa in the Grotto in the dark, and he sits in there with a beard and he pulls you on his lap, whispering all the time. But they came out smiling after they got their presents.

I would not cry in the Grotto even if it was pitch black, and if Santa asked me what I want I would say a kennel for Brock. The shitty pup has wrecked the box and chewed my clothes and still Mam and Kevo don't know he is there. He is getting quieter with the training, he does not bite so much. He is a skinny pup and he sleeps a lot. I got him from the gypsy site. I have trained him as good as I can.

I asked Mam could I see Santa but she said I am too big for that now. She has got the Christmas giro. Maybe she will get me a present this year. My brother Kevo says he will get me an air gun and show me how to aim it at next door's telly.

Yesterday Mam was sick in the toilet. I heard her when I was in bed. Sometimes when she is sick I hold her hand, but there is no room in the toilet to stand next to her. I want to give her a real good present for Christmas, so maybe I will go back to school to make something in the craft lesson. They give you the card and the paints and they even have goldy stuff and Miss Glennie will help you. If I go back I will get in trouble because of wagging off, but I can tell them Mam is sick. This time it is true.

The pup would not go in the door of our flat any more so I tied him up under the stairs. It is dark there and better for him not to be seen. He is better there because of the shit.

My brother Lee has sent a card with a skull and bones on it to Kevo. He says he is coming home soon. He is in Manchester. Sometimes he says he is coming back and he stays away. Maybe he won't come.

Kevo has got a job flogging Christmas trees to people in cars. He says there will be a tree for us on Christmas Eve. I don't remember if we had one before. Last year in the hostel there was one. Carol and Denise, the hostel ladies, put presents on but they weren't real. I broke the lights and Mam slapped me and she had to pay the hostel for the lights mending. But on Christmas Day we got a good dinner and all of us kids played games and some presents were under the tree and this time they were real ones. I got a plastic car transformer from Santa. Mam got bath cubes and soap. Kevo got a pen with a mermaid on it; when you shake it her shells and tail comes on and off. Lee was away that time.

Kevo brought home the Christmas tree and Mam got some snow stuff to put on it.

The pup is dead. Its paws were all chewed off. It did not last as long as the kitten. I think pups are more hard work than cats. And they stink a lot worse. Mam smelt the smell by the stairs and she found the box but it was empty. I put the pup down the chute real fast so she would not know. The box was wet and shitty and Mam saw my clothes in it. She pulled my arm behind my back and dragged me out to the stairs.

"Is this yours?"

"No."

She clouted me. She kicked the box and she yelled.

"You pigging little liar, what was in here, it smells like dead rats..."

I pulled free from her and ran up the stairs and shouted down at her.

"You should know what dead rats smells like..."

Mam does not want Christmas. I have made her a card folded like a crown with a gold angel on. It says 'Happy Christmas from your little angel'. The words were Miss Glennie's idea. I will give it to Mam on Christmas Day, after Santa comes.

I went to Walker Street again. By the Snow White window, I stood for a bit leaning up against the glass with my eyes shut, thinking colours. Dark ones, dull like at the bottom of a well, when the leaves go black and green. Then a hand was shaking my shoulder, and I thought it was the shop man come to see me off for leaning on his window. I opened my eyes. A woman was holding my sleeve. I shoved her off. She held out her hand to me. A note was in her hand. I grabbed the note. I ran and ran until it hurt to breathe. Then I took a good look at it and it was a five pound note. I never had five pounds of my own in my hand before.

I smelt it good. It smelled like shit and metal.

I spit on it for luck. Kissed it like they do in the movies.

I could buy a thing for Mam now, for her Christmas.

I went in the biggest shop, Galloways. Handbags. Gloves. Softy big scarves. Hats. By the perfume counter, the smell was so heavy I felt it pressing on my clothes, going through to my skin. I looked for someone to ask but they all looked away. They closed their blue make-up eyelids and folded up their arms. Their nails were all sharp; painted tiger claws red with blood. Their lips red like they had been dipped in wet blood.

They called a man to throw me out; I showed him my money and he laughed.

"Looka, real leather that is, twenty pounds, nowt under a tenner here, nowt for you so out ye gan."

Five pounds is shit.

What would Shane do?

He would buy a plane ticket and escape. He would buy tabs.

I bought sweets. You can get a load of sweets all right for five pounds.

When I came back home the pup's box was gone.

That was Christmas Eve.

The electric was off. Mam had lit candles. With the tree it was okay, but tomorrow we won't have a good dinner. At the hostel we had turkey and crackers.

Kevo was home and he had a few cans and he sang Christmas carols, but not like Miss Glennie's singing. Like carols were dirty. Then he went out.

Mam says to me, "Michael, I've something to tell you. We're going to have a new bairn..."

"What?"

Her face tries a smile for me, but all that's there is sadness and creases.

"Maybe a little sister for you..."

"Is Da coming back?"

"Ssh. Get to bed now. Be a good boy."

In bed I am cold. If I had punched her belly she would talk. Lee would do that. Kevo shouts and slams the door and her hand shakes. All I do is fetch her tabs and make her tea. Good boy. Go to bed. Once I kicked her chair. Not hard. She slapped me.

She looks different now. The bairn makes her look like that.

A baby brother, crying in my bedroom.
Like the pup, shitting and squealing.
Not like Baby Jesus. Not like Christmas.

Later, I am asleep and Kevo falls in the bed and breaks my sleep. Breathing loud and a drink smell coming off him, he lays all over the bed with his clothes still on. He pushes me to the wall and I feel the cold wall pressing my side. Kevo sticks his knees up and pulls the covers off me. He lies tight, bunched up to jump if the door is hammered. He can be out the window and drop two floors down before I wake up.

"Kevo?"

"Don't you start."

"You know about the bairn?"

"Uhuh… stupid slag."

"When's it coming?"

"Most likely it'll end up like the other one."

"What one?"

Kevo turns over and over in the bed and punches the pillow and pushes me to the wall.

"Before you, like. It died, poor little cunt."

"Died, how?"

He pinches, hard.

"From asking too many questions."

He pinches again, high up my leg by my balls. He pushes me to the wall. Cold against my side.

Kevo is asleep.

Black would be the colour if I could paint my Christmas, not black soft like velvet, but dry black, flat black like the soot on old Babs' kettle down the gypsy site.

I wake up and there is no present from Santa. I look around

and around the room. Under the bed and under Kevo. Nothing.

I go in the kitchen and Lee is there. I drop a plate and he starts. His new belt is off and he's wrapping it around his hand. First thing, before we even sit down to breakfast. Mam says, "Lads, let's have a bit of peace round here now. Can we not enjoy our Christmas for once with no fights."

Lee lets the belt slowly swing from his hand backwards and forwards and the buckle is a head of a wolf with fangs and it drops on the table by me.

"Merry fucking Christmas one and fucking all."

I say, real quiet like, "Why did you come back?"

He says to me dead soft, "None of your fucking cheek, my son."

"I'm never your son."

Mam shouts at me to shut up. Lee hits the belt buckle on the table and sends the milk flying, Mam screams, Kevo wakes up and comes in the kitchen. Sees Lee.

"Back then are yis, ye daft bugger?"

Lee whispers to Kevo and they laugh. Mam makes toast and she gives me a present. It is a square flat thing wrapped in blue paper with stars.

"Sorry, son, it isn't much; best I could do." She holds out her arms to me. I go to kiss her but Lee pulls my hair.

"Soft as shite."

"Why man, let him go, he's only ten," Kevo says. He is in a good mood, he has some cans opened already. I kiss Mam and she holds me to her and I feel her heart beating quickly and she catches her breath and lets me go.

They all watch me opening my present. It is a book. Lee laughs.

"Very pretty! Where d'ye nick that, Ma?"

It is a book for how to bring up a pup. It has pictures, good boys and girls brushing their pups. The pups are fluffy and they do not bite or shit like Brock. I wish Brock was not dead.

"This is shite," Lee shouts out of nowhere, "teaching him to rear pups from a fucking book. Real life is how you learn. *Real life.*" He shouts it in my face.

I go to the bedroom and Kevo follows me in. I look for the thing I made at school. Kevo waits, standing looking out the window.

"That's a nice thing there."

"It's for Mam."

"Very nice. Here."

He gives me a watch.

"Happy Christmas."

I am not to tell Lee about the watch. Kevo does not say this but I know.

We go back to the room. I give Mam her present. It is a gold crown with all glitter and stars on it, as many as I could stick. Most have stayed on. Miss Glennie said it was good. Mam stares and stares at the crown. Lee says, "Put it on, you're the only queen here." Mam slowly, slowly puts it on. It is too big but she holds it with one hand.

"Michael. That's a lovely thing you made me. Thanks, son."

Mam grabs me and squeezes me to her so I smell her face and her sweet smell under her nightie. She kisses me and she rolls a tab, still with the crown on her head, and we laugh. Maybe that was not so black. But just after it got black all right.

Lee puts his can on the floor and I kick it over. I don't see it there, I don't meant to do it.

Lee is worst when he doesn't shout. I see him take the belt off and start to wrap it around his hand, still with the tab in his mouth. He says, dead soft, "Don't move one inch."

Mam is up out of her chair, and pushing me out of the room.

"Get in the toilet, son, lock the door, we'll sort this out, it'll be all right, you'll see." Her crown is falling off and she lets it fall.

Lee is roaring. Kevo goes out. He can't stand up to Lee. Mam calls him not to go but he goes.

I hear the slap of the belt on the kitchen table and Mam talking, pleading like. I hear Lee. I hate this time. I hate Lee. I hate Mam. And the bairn that's coming.

Lee kicks the toilet door. He whacks at the handle with the belt buckle and the noise is so quick and loud I feel the piss jump out of my prick all by itself.

"Come on out of there."

"Mam!"

"She's gone."

"Mam, are you there?"

"Come out before I break the fucking door in..."

He will too. Lee doesn't care this is our home, he doesn't care they told us at the hostel we are on our last chance; he is going to kill me. I hear Mam a long way away, sobbing. I am so scared I even wish Da was back. Then there is hammering at the front door. Police. Lee has his face pushed up against the toilet door and he whispers to me, "If Kevo called them bastards he's dead, after I've done with you."

"Open up!"

I think Lee grabs Mam. He likes to twist arms, maybe that is what he does. Mam is dead quiet.

"Open up in there!"

"Don't do it, Maureen..."

"If you don't open this door we'll break it down..."

Lee is beaten. He hates that the worst thing. I hear Mam opening the door. He says, "Micka, you hear me? If you get me in shite for this, you'll pay for it."

I put my hand over my face and squeeze. It is hard to breathe. I am not crying, there is water coming out of my eyes, but it is not crying if you keep quiet.

Then two police is in the flat and Mam is telling them I am locked in the toilet. They knock on my door.

"What's his name? Come on out of there, Michael. Haway, lad."

I open the door. Lee's belt has disappeared by magic. He has a greasy smile on, he pats me on the head. Mam does a fake laugh for the police. One looks at me. One looks at Lee, up and down, up and down.

"I'll check this lock for you."

The police is checking the lock. Lee is looking at me, Mam is looking at me. I have this lump of stuff in my chest. This hard thing that hurts all the way up to my throat. My jeans are wet. I am crying. Lee folds his arms and stares at me.

"We had a complaint of noise..."

"Sorry, officer," Mam says, stroking my hair, "we might have got a bit merry..."

"Said it sounded like someone was being hit. Did anyone hit you, Michael?"

"No."

I see Lee nod. I have said the right thing. We must not shop Lee, he is family.

"They must have made a mistake," Mam says.

Old cop gives me a hanky to wipe my face.

"We're in the neighbourhood. If we hear any more complaints we'll be round again," he says to Lee. Lee is grinning back. Not a care in the world now.

They go away down the corridor. Mam says,

"Show the officers out, Michael."

By the door the young one stops.

"Here."

He gets a shiny thing from his uniform pocket and gives it me.

"It's a harmonica. You can play canny tunes on it."

The older one shakes his head, "Haway, man, don't waste your breath."

Young one bends down and whispers.

"Happy Christmas, bonny lad."

They are gone.

Something inside me is tearing. It tears as easy as wet paper.

The Merchant's Tale

David Darton

I am seen where I am not,

I am heard where eyes is not,

Tell me now what I am,

and see that you misse me not

A riddle

The trader's name was Jack. He liked the tag 'Jack the Lad'. Ever on the lookout for a quick quid. Wheeling and dealing, moving from place to place. And as the main reward for his endeavours, enjoying pleasures of the flesh; never with guilt or remorse. Although there were some downers when deals went sour, he had fun too. Like this day, down the market, flogging – in a pretty good American accent – the latest invention that he'd brought (personally, of course) across the Atlantic all the way from the USA, especially for you good people.

The lady didn't buy. But he noticed her. Standing in the bright November cold. First, across the road. Later, further along on the corner. Not his usual type. Taller and with darker hair and colouring than the petite English roses that normally got his pulse racing. But a striking face, even at a distance. And a body poised as though it knew itself and its needs well. Eventually, as he was starting to pack up for the day, she approached. "Well, siree, in old Mississippi this stuff is yesterday." The accent was only a little better than his.

Later in bed he lay spent. Twice. She was fun. He wanted more of this.

Why did the telephone always ring just as you were about to sit down to eat? Mrs Dale moved her still-sprightly self down the long hall of Old Monk House that she and Mr Dale had run as a luxury guest house in Jesmond for thirty years.

"Hello, Old Monk House."

"Is that Mrs Dale?" An odd accent. American, but from a different place than any of the many American guests she had had over the years. She smiled.

"Yes."

"We wondered if you had any rooms available from next Friday?"

"I'm sorry, we're closed in February. It's the month there are fewest visitors you see and at my age I need the rest and a chance to see to the house. Especially since my husband passed away."

"Oh. I'm sorry." Disappointment. "We were really hoping to come and stay. A friend of ours, Harry Bottomsby – you might remember, the insurance agent. He stayed last year. Well, he told us how wonderful your place was with history pouring from every room. We have always wanted to explore Northumberland and Tyneside. My husband and I are social historians and my ancestors come from the North East..." She paused, "It's the only chance we have to spend a few weeks soaking up the atmosphere and exploring. And I just hate staying in anonymous hotels."

A few weeks. Most people stayed only a few days. "Well, I suppose if you are that keen. There's just me and my daughter, June, here – she's helping out doing some jobs for a couple of weeks. You'd have to look after yourselves…"

She replaced the receiver. Her step was much lighter as she returned to the kitchen. June raised her eyebrows. Mrs Dale nodded.

Jack grinned at April, which, incongruously, her name turned out to be. Not anywhere near a strong enough name for her. He was still having lots of fun – they had just had a quick fumble and rush of lust in the near-empty carriage after the train disgorged most passengers at York. But he wasn't at all sure about this particular adventure. Jack hadn't really understood why she picked him up in the first place. He had an uneasy feeling it might all have been leading to this.

"Well, at least we will get a couple of weeks in a nice place," April was saying as the train slowed for Newcastle Central. "By the way, I didn't tell you. You know her daughter who is staying with her? Guess what her name is? June. Two months *behind* me. But then no one is ever able to get *ahead* of my scheming." She laughed hard. April never just giggled.

As the taxi climbed the slope from the city centre for the short ride to Jesmond, old Victorian terraces gave way to grander mansions and a leafier feel.

Jesmond turned out to be a haven of tranquillity, but it was through the city centre and the vibrant quayside that Jack wandered, sometimes with April, sometimes alone, soaking up the banter and energy of the city. Jack found himself not bored, as he had feared he would be, but drawn into a romance with the place that was an alien experience for him. Old Monk House itself was spectacular and the perfect foil after a day in the city.

One evening, June was showing him the garden. "It seems idyllic here," she said, "but it has been a hard life really for my mum. We can only afford staff when tourism is booming. It's got even harder since the regeneration of the riverside and all the new luxury hotels that have opened in the last fifteen years. Then there are periods when Americans aren't travelling because of one international catastrophe or another. Although Newcastle is not high on their list, it makes a difference at the margin. I know it's kind of luxurious here and quite expensive to stay, but it doesn't really make the finances work much better – Old Monk House isn't really big enough to make a fortune. And my mum and dad have expensive tastes. They like nice things around them, you know. My mum's tired now; even meeting new people all the time – one of the things she really liked – is a strain now. She needs to retire." Jack saw a tear form and couldn't help brush it away. June smiled and her face seemed to him to light up magnificently despite her sadness. He was surprised to find himself feeling sad too. It was a long time since he had felt empathy of this sort with someone else.

Later, he was with April. Her brashness seemed sometimes to jar here. But he still craved the excitement of her. No night was the same.

At all levels, it seemed, he was allowing himself to be led by his feelings rather than by calculated design for gain, despite the reason they were now here. It was intoxicating. And he found himself less and less able to restrict his feelings to April.

There was this one night. The here and now. She understood his new needs. She stood naked, silhouetted against the moonlit window in what would have been a celluloid cliché except for the sublime contentment that ran through him. He moved to her, his arousal rising. This wasn't sex as before. Jack knew from the first touch of this encounter that this was a joining of two flowing tributaries into one magnificent river. As his tongue slipped from neck to breast and back and around and lower. As her full mouth devoured every nerve ending in an endless spreading of heat. As their lips met and parted and explored and met again. As their hands and tongues flowed in caresses that merged together until the two of them were undivided.

"Liquid fire," he whispered as the most intense yet relaxed finishing washed over him and into her.

"It looks like the real McCoy," Jack said, looking at the carver in one of the reception rooms. "Sixteenth century, probably by one of the Huguenot craftsmen that came over here after the persecutions in Europe."

"You're more educated than you let on, aren't you," laughed April.

"Well actually, I went up to Cambridge before becoming a barrow boy," he said, switching from what had become a painful American accent to his best Oxbridge tones. "But I was too restless for the City," his voice relaxing into the East End of his childhood. "And there's only so far a bloke can go in faking the 'born to it' easiness which is necessary really to get on there." He sounded bitter.

"I still have much to learn about you, don't I, lover boy?" She gave him a playful kiss and slap on the bum. He relaxed into a laugh. Things had changed between them since the liquid fire encounter. Nevertheless, fun was still fun, even if it now felt somehow obligatory and that something was missing. What he really sought now was to repeat that night. But the circumstances hadn't been right… In the meantime his loins still demanded. They turned to head upstairs.

"Anyway, old Bottomsby was right," she said, as they headed towards the door to the hall. "There's a fortune in this house – and I know someone who can sell it on if we get hold of it." She saw the doubt in his face. "It's all trade at the end of the day, and profit is fair. I mean, she's bound to be insured. Look at this vase. It almost looks like Ming Dynasty or something."

"It's not," said Mrs Dale, coming through the door from the dining room and startling them, "but it is pretty isn't it? Seventeenth century Persian. Quite valuable, my late husband said when he had it insured. I just liked it, but it seems what I liked was always a good investment too. So that was good, wasn't it?" She smiled.

Jack wondered what Mrs Dale had overheard. But she was quite deaf. She probably just heard the comment about the vase as she actually came into the room. After all, she was no actress and seemed quite at ease.

They excused themselves and made a run for the bedroom before getting into another disjointed recollection of long ago that old women like Mrs Dale seemed to have an unlimited stock of. As he watched April go up the stairs in front of him, he wondered…Knows someone who can fence stolen property. Can organise a robbery. He wondered if he should be afraid of her.

They were all having tea together in one of the drawing rooms, enjoying the last of the day's watery sun. Jack and April were together on the sofa, June and her mother on chairs opposite.

Jack considered the two younger women. Very different. April strong, fun and vibrant. June slimmer, more classically beautiful, sensuous and less inclined to get fired up in conversation. Maybe the difference was what created the tension. Or maybe it was the more normal issue of…

"I shall be leaving on Tuesday," said June, interrupting his thoughts.

"What a shame," gushed April in her best southern drawl. A distinct pause. "For your mother."

A fixed smile from June.

"More tea?" said Mrs Dale sweetly, her mind coming back from wherever it had been.

Jack looked at the two younger women. He had never really betrayed anyone before. He felt the first pangs of doubt.

"Thank goodness for that," said April, as they strolled round the gardens in the last of the afternoon light. "I thought she was going to stick around and we would have to make an excuse to stay beyond Friday. This place is amazing, isn't it? Just made for lifting stuff. That wall around the guest parking area will block the view of the vans completely. We'll set up the drivers for Thursday evening."

"But how will we get Mrs Dale out of the place?" Jack countered. "She's hardly left it since we arrived. The one time she and June left as we were going out, they switched on the alarm system. And you know it's state of the art, linked to the local cop shop."

"Ah, ye man of little faith. I have a plan. It just requires you to be able to fake sickness. Shouldn't be too difficult. After all, you're a man." Her uproarious laugh broke the peace of the evening as she poked him in the ribs.

April helped Mrs Dale up out of her seat. The much acclaimed performance she had just sat through was *so* tedious. But she smiled and gushed as required.

"It was so good of you to come with me. Y'all know how much I hate coming to things like this on my own. I half think Jack was faking being ill because this sort of thing is really not his thing, you know. But I'm probably being unfair. Such luck that you're so fond of Chekhov. I'm not really. It's just the sort of thing I feel one should do, especially in England."

"He was Russian."

"I know, I know. But y'all know that it's not often we get the chance to see anything like this back home. Being here makes you want to, you know, improve yourself. Anyway, lucky that you're so keen on him."

April looked up at the clock. "Is that all it is. I thought it was later. Not that I didn't enjoy it, you know. It's just that..." Suddenly she fell sharply down the three steps leading from the foyer to the street doors.

"Aaargh, my ankle," she yelled through gritted teeth.

"You're sure you'll be alright?" said Mrs Dale anxiously at Accident and Emergency.

"Yes, you get on home. It's late and they say it may take a couple of hours as they're busy. Tell Jack I'll get a taxi back later. The pain is easing already. Honest."

"Alright, if you're sure. I don't like being out this late really, you know."

Jack should have left straight after the lads finished loading the vans. That was what he had agreed with April. But he suddenly felt ill. Really ill, not fake ill. Probably tension. He sat for a while and then went to the cloakroom near the front door. He retched, but little came up. As he was recovering, Jack heard the front door open. Oh Christ, April had promised to keep Mrs Dale occupied until at least eleven o'clock, whatever she had to do.

But it wasn't her. It was a man's step, passing the cloakroom, heading down to the kitchen, not the slow shuffle of Mrs Dale. Jack stayed where he was. He heard noises from the kitchen, but not the closing of the kitchen door into the hall. He couldn't escape unseen. He waited.

After a few minutes, the front door opened again. Lighter footsteps. Then:

"Champagne? Well, I suppose we deserve it." June? A man laughed. The front door opened again.

"Hello?" Mrs Dale. Jack looked at his watch. Just on eleven o'clock.

"In here, Mum." Definitely June.

"Mmm…champagne." Mrs Dale sounded younger somehow and her walk down the hall brisker. The kitchen door closed.

Jack quietly headed to the front door. But then curiosity got the better of him; he turned and went and stood by the kitchen door, listening.

"Well here's to you Mr Dale," said Mrs Dale, "or should I say Mr Bottomsby." Laughter all round.

"What saps, it worked better than we could ever have hoped," said Mr Dale.

"I'd better make the call and get that April picked up. I palmed one of my necklaces onto her at the theatre in case she tries to wriggle out of it. We need someone who will be convincing with the insurance company that it was antiques that were stolen. I'll use the phone in the dining room." Jack heard her leave.

"And here's a toast to you for using your charms so effectively young lady."

"Thanks Dad."

"But I'm still not sure why you took the risk."

"We needed Jack to confide in me. Now we know where the vans are going for the night, I've arranged for…well, you don't want to know, but insurance companies often have informers among criminals, and they must never discover that they weren't real antiques. Antiques!" She laughed. "Mum told me that that stupid woman thought our vase from the Selfridges sale was Ming!"

"And then we dump Jack," said her father. "You didn't actually have to… you know…"

"No, of course not Dad. He just needed romancing. And don't worry, he knows nothing about you and Mum setting up the robbery, or the fact that you're Mr Bottomsby."

Jack felt sick again.

"How's the fencing of the real stuff going?" June continued.

"It's all done my love. We've got nearly half a million pounds. And now the insurance will give us another three-quarters of a million. It will clear my debts and give us a new start."

"And Dad…"

"I know. No more casinos or horses. I promise."

"Where the hell is he?" April paced up and down outside the hospital. She had texted Jack to tell him about the fake accident necessary to create delay and told him to meet her here instead.

"Come on, Jack," she muttered.

"Are you Mrs April Honeyman?"

She spun round to face the man and his upheld police shield. The colour drained from her. If Jack had double-crossed her... No one did that to her and survived. She looked from him to his colleague and back. Then shrugged.

"Is there a problem?"

"Well, some accusations have been made by a Mrs Dale. We are getting increasingly hysterical calls from her...You have been staying at Old Monk House, haven't you?"

April couldn't for the moment answer, though she knew there was no point in denying it. She would be able to blame Jack and say she had nothing to do with it.

"If you are not going to answer here, I think you'd better come with us."

Jack heard a muffled voice and then "Coming dear" from Mr Dale and the sound of him going out towards the dining room. Jack had been frozen outside the door, but now slowly opened it.

June's hand flew to her mouth. "Out!" she hissed, rushing over and half pushing him back through the door. She looked at his deflated self.

"I had to reassure my parents that I have not put them at risk by telling you about it all – Dad being Mr Bottomsby and so on – and I didn't want to tell you earlier because it may have changed the way you related to Mum."

She looked at him intensely and then leaned up and kissed his neck. "Don't worry. I felt the liquid fire too."

June closed the kitchen door and propelled him towards the front door. She pressed her lips softly to his. "I have to sort out my parents and then I'll come for you in a couple of weeks like we arranged. Now go." She reached behind him and unlatched the front door.

Standing outside in the cold drizzle, he stared at the closed house. For two women, he had now trodden a route against his better judgement. Had they just seduced him to use him?

But it was liquid fire, wasn't it? And June had just said she felt it too. As April had said, no one but an insurance company was going to suffer. Except now, of course, April. June had never told him that setting her up was part of the plan.

He tried to walk away with confidence in his step, burying his doubts very deep down. June would come for him. He would feel the flowing river again.

"Lovely rugs, these!" he called to the passing trade. "Brought personally for you all the way from Persia."

But the old Jack the Lad gift of the gab had left him.

June had said she would come for him within a few weeks. That was three months ago. Last weekend he had trekked back up to Newcastle. Old Monk House was now boarded up.

Jack sighed.

Would June really come now after all this time?

Worse, would April come for him?

The Motorist's Tale

Astrid Hymers

Whisht lads haad yor gobs

an aal tell yer an aaful story

(Listen lads, keep quiet,

while I tell you an awful story)

An old Tyneside folksong

"You're listening to Radio Newcastle with Jon Harle taking you up to seven o'clock. For drivers homeward bound with the prospect of a fine weekend ahead, we're bringing you up to date with the latest traffic news. Drivers are advised to find alternative routes north and south towards the Tyne Bridge, where traffic has reached a standstill due to a serious incident."

The lorry alongside, windows down, was tuned into the same station, the volume high enough to render Tony's car radio superfluous. A hot weekend was forecast, but now, in the rush hour, the air was humid, the sky dull and overcast, threatening thunder. Even though he'd run the windows down trying to catch any hint of a breeze, the air hung still and heavy, his shirt clung damply to his back, hands clammy on the steering wheel.

Three lines of traffic tailed back from the roundabout at the foot of Gateshead's High Street towards Low Fell, and ahead Tony saw vehicles converging from all directions, engines idling, fumes adding to the oppressive atmosphere, a complete gridlock.

The lorry, its diesel engine throbbing noisily through the open windows, inched forward until almost touching the bumper of the car in front. With nothing better to do, Tony glanced up towards the cab where the driver sat, big, beefy and sweating in a grubby singlet emblazoned with 'Toon Army'.

The radio DJ's voice cut in again.

"This is an urgent traffic announcement for drivers accessing the Tyne Bridge north and south of the river. Police advise you take alternative routes. The Tyne Bridge will be closed until further notice due to an attempted suicide."

"Fucking marvellous! Divven't these nutters have nowt better to do?"

Tony got an earful of the string of obscenities through the

lorry's open window. The driver was thumping his fist against the steering wheel, perspiration trickling down his face and glistening wetly on his hairy chest.

"Yer drive all the way from fucking Folkstone and a mile from fucking home some daft sod decides to top hisself and buggers up everything. How the hell can yer take another route when yer stuck nose to arse?" He gave a noisy blast on the air horn as if to emphasise his point.

With less of the road rage, Tony was thinking almost the same. Tonight of all nights he wanted to be home on time. Sort things out with Andrew. Not for the first time he wished Lynne was there to resolve situations like this – back him up, calm the atmosphere. Even two years on, his body still ached for her. Thinking of Lynne brought a lump to his throat. Hot tears spilled unchecked. Embarrassed, he brushed them hurriedly away. What would the dickhead of a lorry driver make of a grown man crying?

Just when things had been looking up, his life had all gone pear-shaped. He and Lynne had been childhood sweethearts, school friends, best mates. Weathering life's ups and downs together. With good prospects at the shipyard, they'd planned happily for the future. Gutted when Swan's had gone to the wall and for the first time in his life he'd been on the dole, she'd been more than ready to get a job in the supermarket to help make ends meet, encouraging him to retrain. It hadn't been easy, what with the two kids, but they'd managed. He smiled remembering the pair of them dancing madly round the kitchen and opening a bottle of plonk when he'd got the job at Nissan. Things were really rosy, new car, canny lifestyle, the odd holiday abroad...until the Big C bombshell. His beautiful Lynne. They'd been stunned, shattered. How would they tell the kids?

Oasis was blasting out 'Champagne Super Nova' when the DJ interrupted.

"Just a further traffic update. Drivers are urged to find alternative routes to avoid the Tyne Bridge. Police and rescue services are trying to talk down a teenage boy who is threatening to throw himself off the bridge..."

"Stupid little shit!"

Tony turned to see the lorry driver's angry face, now more of a pucey colour, his black hair plastered by sweat to his face and neck, yelling at no one in particular.

"Yer put in a hard day's graft, look forward to a pint, yer fish and chips, a bit of footie on the telly and some daft bastard screws it up!"

Throat like sandpaper, Tony fumbled in the glove compartment searching for sweets left over by the kids and found a screwed up packet containing a few Love Hearts. Lauren...sweet kid. The love of his life. A 'mammy's girl', she'd taken Lynne's death really badly. Turning to Tony in her grief, he'd done his best to comfort her and consequently found solace himself. Poor kid, at thirteen she was becoming quite the little housewife. Not fair, he knew, but Lauren never complained. A bit like Lynne...

But then there was Andrew. Defiant, insolent, sullen. He and Lynne had such great hopes for both their kids. Bright and intelligent, they'd both done well at school, though Lynne had not lived to see Andrew's exam successes.

It had been hard for the lad, trying to cram and take exams while his mam was so ill. Lynne would have been proud of Andrew. Eventually, they'd had to move her to the hospice and it broke them in pieces.

In sixth form he'd begun well, then the trouble started. Sullen silences lasting for days. Late nights, bad company. The perpetual rows when he sloped in after midnight stinking of booze in blatant defiance of times laid down for getting home. Last night had been the worst. They'd gone at each other's throats, throwing blame and recrimination back and forth.

"All you think of is yourself!" yelled Andrew, his voice broken and low, face flushed. "You're not the only one who misses Mam. But you moon around as though Lauren and me aren't here. No wonder I'd rather be with my mates, 'cos you think nobody should be happy." He was a strapping six foot, and with a shock, Tony realised he wasn't a kid any more. There were the first signs of downy facial hair and he made a mental note to introduce him to a razor. Desperation at Andrew's continuing defiance had his tongue running away. He heard himself wading into the kid, telling him he was a selfish, ungrateful young pup. He was working all hours to feed and clothe them, keep a roof over their heads. Lauren was doing her bit, but what the hell was Andrew doing except roaming the streets till all hours, getting up to God knows what, under-age drinking and, for all he knew, dabbling in drugs?

All the pent-up heartache, sorrow and distress he'd thrown at the boy. He wanted to hurt him as he still hurt...and succeeded with his parting shot, "What would your mam think?" His fists had clenched, wanting to hit him as they'd eyeballed each other. Andrew seemed to crumple and looked ready to cry, but managed to say, "I hate you Dad! Hit me and I'll report you!" And then, barely audible, "I wish I were dead."

Lauren burst into tears and ran to her room, slamming the door and, without another word, Andrew followed suit.

Tony was up early for his journey to Washington, his eyes dry and red following a sleepless night. Lauren sat quietly having breakfast as he prepared their packed lunches. He dropped a kiss on the top of her tousled hair.

"See you later sweetheart. Maybe if it's a fine night we can go down to Whitley Bay for a change. Have a pizza or something?"

She nodded enthusiastically and hugged him, "Love you Dad."

He could smell the newly washed freshness of her hair, the scent of her skin. Her warmth tugged at his heart. Of Andrew there was no sign. He'd have to have it out with him tonight. Find out what was at the bottom of it all. Maybe the lad was right and he was wrapped up in his own misery.

Kylie was giving 'I should be so lucky' one hundred percent when the DJ's voice cut in...

"Traffic has been brought to a standstill and there are five-mile tailbacks north and south of the Tyne Bridge as police and rescue workers try to talk down a teenage lad from the superstructure of the bridge."

"For Christ's sake! I'm missing the toon match. Get it over with, yer stupid bastard. Jump and let's all get home."

The lorry driver spluttered spittle across his windscreen and again gave vent on the horn.

Tony turned away in disgust. It was somebody's kid after all. Mixed up. Hormones haywire. At odds with his family...

A shiver ran down his spine as though someone had walked over his grave. His knuckles turned white as he grasped the steering wheel. It couldn't be...

A Tale of Memory; the Tail of Love

Michael Pattison

Plants, parks and gardens never stop

changing, by day, by season or by year.

We have restored the park, but now we have

to let it grow. The next few years are

going to be exciting and challenging.

Adam Greenwold

Unforgettable.

A summer of passion, of lust, of love.

And now it was all over. We lay there in the grass, overshadowed by that falsity of male dominance: St James's Park, dwarfing and destroying the natural bliss of Leazes Park beneath it.

Silence.

Oh, the *silences*! They spoke more than our words. The looks. The *looks*. Long, lasting looks of longing love.

Lament. Lament that it was now over. Or soon to be.

"Why must time exist?" I asked.

"If it didn't exist," she replied, "there'd be no anticipation. Nothing to look forward to."

"It shouldn't exist. It *shouldn't*." Like a spoilt child.

In fact, when we *were* together, it *didn't* exist. Time merely prolonged our minds when apart: the fears, the desires, the racing excitement, the highs and the lows; but when we were together there was no time. There was no past, no future, no present. Only the moment. Only the instant. Only the eternal abyss of existence. An existence of spontaneity and of immeasurable desire. Galaxies apart and yet our bodies were one.

We lay there, looking into each other's eyes. Sometimes she smiled. To ease the pain. It didn't. I didn't smile. *Couldn't* smile. Seriousness. A grave certainty that this was the last time. We kissed.

Kissed. Each time it got better, magnifying the loneliness to come. Her eyes closed, her tongue gentle, her nails gliding across my neck and through my hair. Every amazing flash between us; the moment, the magnificence, the memories. All put into that one kiss. Like *every* kiss. She was the epicentre of my emotional earthquake.

"I don't want you to leave," I said. It was a silly thing to say. Like a doomed holocaust victim pleading to live. I looked away and lay down on my back. Birds overhead. Oblivious to the turmoil around and below them. I envied them endlessly; their freedom, their elegance, their ability to become art at any moment.

"Then come with me." She'd said it before, countless times. She brought her face over mine, cutting out the sunlight. So I could look into her eyes without squinting.

I simply sighed. *You know I can't.*

"Why?" she asked.

"You know why; I've told you." I looked away again, putting my head to the side. Looking along the nap of the grass and wishing I could become it. Lifeless grass, without love, without worry, without anguish. It *welcomed* being cut down. It relished its own death, for it was in death that it found neatness and beauty. While humans wasted away...

I couldn't leave. Tyneside; the centre of my world. I loved her. But I also loved *her*. We'd spent the summer together; it had gone *beyond* intimate. But if time was the greatest of all measures, it was a mere fling. Nothing compared to the lifelong bond with home.

"You must remember to write every day," I told her. *Reminded* her. I'd forgotten how many times.

"I will, I will." An attempt to reassure, but words meant nothing.

It was just us. The world did not exist. Our only company was two stone lions, sitting symmetrically on the grass with us, statues of life. I closed my eyes and pretended to be dead. Held my breath. She noticed and slapped me on the face. A playful slap. It didn't hurt. She smiled. I closed my eyes again.

"You're silly, you know that."

"How come?"

"Not moving away with me. You say you love me in one breath, and that you won't move away with me in another."

"You don't understand."

"Then make me."

"I can't," I snapped back. Sighed. "Words cannot express it."

"What are you going to do?"

"I don't know" – I didn't know – "perhaps I'll write a novel. A *short* novel. I get bored with lengthy ones. Especially when you're around. I can't concentrate long enough."

"Then write a novel," she said, as if that was that, and all things were dandy and sorted. "A short novel."

"I don't know." A pause. A violent pause. They were all violent. Violently exhausting. "My prose sucks. I hate it. I can't write fiction. I can only write about you."

"You're blind, you know," she said, as if diagnosing me with cancer.

"What do you mean?"

"This isn't the place to be. You're going to write, but you'll never get published. Or you said last week you'd make a film. But that would never be funded. You should move away with me. London is the place where it's all happening. Not here."

"You see! Now *you're* blind. People need to open their eyes. There is more to England than red buses and rhyming slang. People cringe and shudder at the thoughts of the grey skies and green fields of the north. If only they forgot their self-importance for a day or two and came up here. *Then* they'd see."

"What would they see?"

"I don't know. Friendliness. Taste. Life. It's all chaotic down there. Fancy a city where the most famous place is where people go to satisfy their sexual insecurities."

"*Soho* isn't the most famous place in London."

I ignored her. "When you say you're from Tyneside, everybody says, 'Wey aye man,' in that hideous southern imitation. I've never heard anybody from up *here* say that though. Never. Never in all my life. 'Wey aye man.' It's so clichéd. So archaic. So not here."

"It's a mark of identity, though, isn't it," she suggested. "It's the way by which people recognise you."

"*Exactly*. That's why it stinks of bollocks. Why recognise somebody by something which is actually very rarely said?"

I held her and she kissed me. It was nonsense. It'd gone over her head. It was alright for *her*. She was going to be devoured by art school and culture. Culture. What a pathetic word. If you were against culture you were racist, and if you were for culture you were a moron. There was no in-between. No wonder we'd failed the Culture Bid. It was hideous: the campaign, the ideas, the whole initial concept in the first place.

"Then write about *me*," she said, moving on, or moving back, whichever way you looked at it. "When I'm gone."

"Perhaps I will. There's a short story competition coming up. I never usually go in for them. Traditionalist morons from the south usually win. But perhaps this one will be different."

"What will you write about?"

"I don't know. Perhaps I'll write about my affair."

"Affair?" She was intrigued. "Go on."

"With two people. One's divine, an absolute goddess. She is the air I breathe, the food I eat, the film I watch, the poetry I read. She is the grass I lie on right now, the birds circling above me, the clouds passing overhead. She is the embodiment of life, and everything I wish for from it."

She was smiling. Immune to my poetic frankness. The smile was a knowing one; almost mocking, as if my pretentiousness wasn't to be taken seriously. But deep down she knew. She *knew*.

"And the other?" she asked.

"The goddess is real, and I can see her now. Feel her now. *Be* her now. But the other person is intangible, elusive. Neither a he nor a she. It is a *place*. A place of life, of a buzzing excitement which pleases me in every other way the first girl cannot. It's awful, to be so attached to a place. Like Woody Allen, in the opening of *Manhattan*, when he says, 'He adored New York City; he idolised it all out of proportion.' I feel the same. It's not in my heart. It's deeper than that. It's in my gut, in my loins, in my soul. It's all around me. It envelops me like a hot fire. No, a *warm* fire. A comforting one."

"I'll be glad to leave."

"Leave *me*?"

"No, silly." She gestured to slap me again. "To leave *here*. I don't see things in it what you do."

"Because you're *looking*. I'm not. That's why I can never leave this place."

Like Allen in New York, with a country between himself and Hollywood, I would stay. Stay and change the world from this modest life of growing importance. It was too easy to move south to make it big. Everybody did it. They betrayed their backgrounds in exchange for experience and pompousness.

She was staring at me. I could tell, as I lay there fiddling with a blade of grass. I met her gaze. She was serious. All very serious all very sudden. A child realising her mother's reprimand isn't a joke. Realising that she is just like the rest of us. Mortal. Life too short, the world too small. *Le temps détruit tout*. Of course. Sure. Wey aye man.

We kissed again, and this time she was crying. I held her tight and close, like my life depended on it. It was an aggressive, reassuring kiss. *Remember to write*. She would. But not forever. It would fizzle out. And she knew it. And so did I. Our subconscious fears fighting to spoil the moment.

But they couldn't.

For the world spun on its axis as it always did. St James's Park still stood there, proud and redundant; the birds still circled overhead, oblivious and stress-free; the grass was still intensely green in the sunshine; the stone lions still sat at either side like fiercely loyal guards, looking on into eternity. And together they shaped the moment, the magnificence, the memory.

Unforgettable.

Natalya's Tale

Carol McGuigan

...we have no control over our place of birth,

but we live with the consequences forever.

Alan Plater

Natalya sniffs at the bucket. The blue plastic smells chemical, of a world that hates human beings. She lifts it into the big sluice sink and begins to fill it with water. She dabbles her fingers under the tap till it gets too hot. She should be wearing gloves.

Shona and Julie waved a pair at her when she started last month. She might have thought this was kindness but they didn't show her 'Supply'. Supply is the cupboard full of gloves, mops, buckets and pretty much everything you need for the job. Bill showed it to her in her second week, proudly opening the door at the end of his fire exit tour. She dumped the metal bucket she'd bought new from the market and chose this lighter one. "Goes with your eyes," Bill said. The water reaches the brim.

Natalya feels hot from the steam and from thinking about how she clanked up and down with that first heavier bucket while Julie and Shona laughed in their hands. She turns on the cold tap and moves the bucket aside. She puts her hands under the freezing water and lets it run for a while, then lifts her hands to her face. Her cold wet palms cool her cheeks. This could be the heat that comes with the change. She's forty now. She watches the gushing torrent then slowly twists off the tap. She dries her hands with a cloth, wiping each finger, no rings to put back now.

Julie and Shona laugh just outside the main door. Natalya quickly lifts up the bucket. She likes to get going before they arrive but this morning she's too late.

Steeling herself, she carries the bucket awkwardly into the hall and heads toward the lift. Shona and Julie fall silent. Maybe Bill has told them to 'pack it in'. He used this expression about stopping smoking. The lift doors open on him, standing like a tree, his arms held out to each wall. His face falls when he sees her. He isn't even whistling.

"Y'all right Natalya?" He looks worried.

"Yes I'm fine." She tries to keep her voice steady.

He nods and looks over her head at the other two women, raising his voice to include them. "I was watching that News ' 24. About the school in Russia."

Natalya turns to see Shona nodding; saddened and still.

"Terrible," Bill says.

"Terrible," Shona agrees.

Bill shakes his head, "All them bairns they've got captive."

"They want shootin'," Julie fires back.

Bill's eyes screw up in baffled rage.

The bucket's plastic handle feels hard against Natalya's hand. She coughs. Bill steps to one side in the lift. "Haway in pet."

Natalya enters and the doors close swiftly. Bill presses the fourth floor button.

"It's not where you're from is it?"

Natalya looks up at him, puzzled.

"That Belsan, Beslan I mean." His face is full of concern.

"No," she replies; "I'm from Moscow."

"Moscow, that's right." Bill nods to himself. "Not really near to it then?"

Natalya shakes her head.

"Right." Bill looks uncertain.

The lift arrives at the fourth floor.

Bill asks quickly, before she gets out, "Still all right for tonight?"

Natalya feels something give at his whisper. "Yes," she tells him gently. She smiles at him and carries the steaming water into the corridor. The lift closes.

Natalya's heart weighs as much as the bucket. She wants to hear Bill whistling. She wipes invisible grime from stainless steel windows in a room full of switched off computers.

"From Russia with Love," he sang, the first time they spoke, surprised she didn't know it. "James Bond?" he tried again, shaking his head.

Next day he brought in a postcard picture of a film star, tanned and in a tuxedo. He pointed at himself. "Geordie James Bond?"

Natalya laughed. It's his gift to her.

The market stall is a bank of colour and shapes. Natalya silently practises asking for beetroot. She sometimes forgets the words. Some, like orange and onion, are closer to the French. She hadn't expected that. Beetroot. Sounds like 'Be True'. She caresses the stacked potatoes, still earthy from the soil, feeling the goodness of dirt.

"Yes love." A woman with scraped back hair looks expectantly.

"Be True," Natalya says.

But the woman understands.

Putin's face appears on seven screens in the TV shop window. Natalya stands mesmerised. It's strange to see her president so clearly in this Newcastle street. The big wide screens make things look so real but also more like a movie. There's no sound and she can't quite lip-read but she can guess what he's saying.

"He has a strategy," Pavel would say, as if such plans were sacred.

Natalya would point to the stories she'd read in the paper. Pavel would patiently listen. He would hold his palm out towards her, "They don't want peace. They're terrorists." His eyes so clear and calm. He would kiss her forehead and then drive to the lab. She would brood with her migraine and coffee.

She forces herself to pull away from Putin. His black coat and ashen face rehearsing once more for death, not his own, of course. She makes herself check her shopping. The brown paper bags, full of vegetables, need to be taken home. She straightens and then senses the watching. She feels more flattered than disturbed, especially in her flat shoes and old bulky coat. Maybe she's not so middle-aged. She grew to feel her curves were too much for Pavel who liked things trim and reserved but with Bill she feels almost delicate, not that he's seen her naked. But who would watch her all the way down the street? Behind her are only two skinny young men, wearing the black and white football shirts that seem to be uniform, and an old headscarved woman, like a babushka from home. Natalya walks to the bus stop, shoulders tense from the bags. She looks round once on the bus, knowing it to be silly, that she's tired from the six o'clock start. There's no one there, of course.

She chops the onions. Fine white lines run through each layer, like the notepaper Pavel wrote on late into the night. She would watch him from the doorway, see his head bent over.

"Soon," he would promise when she stood there in her nightdress. "I'll come to bed very soon," he would nod, smiling, but then bend again to his work.

The hours ticked away and she'd fall asleep alone. One morning she leafed through his writing. What could be so captivating? Pages of symbols and chemical formulae. But she knew his technician job frustrated him, that these pages were steps towards a better future, a research post maybe.

Natalya's eyes sting and she stops chopping. Reaching for a tea towel, she hears the news from the radio. The reporter describes the scene at the siege. A thousand held in the school gymnasium. She breathes in hard through her nostrils and opens the door to the balcony, stepping out into the cold but clean-smelling air. She tries not to picture the gunmen. She can't believe there'll be women there this time. Those black-clad young widows. Pavel would have seen them, with their legs wrapped round explosives in memory of their husbands. She shakes her head free of the images and looks hard at the blank North East English sky. This is where she is. After a moment, she returns to the kitchen, letting the brisk outsideness flow into the flat. She fiddles with the radio and finds music. No more news tonight.

Natalya sees Bill's tall, bulky shadow through the frosted glass. He's turning away, as if surveying her neighbourhood. She smoothes the velvet of her dress, fingers still pink from the borscht. As she opens the door, the breeze from the balcony ruffles the back of her hair. Bill turns to face her.

"Wow!" he says quietly, he seems to be blushing. He's wearing a shirt and tie under his zip-up jacket.

Natalya fears she's made too much effort. At work she never wears make-up. He'll think her desperate now.

"I see you've got cameras." Bill hovers on the doorstep and nods out at the estate. "CCTV," he says.

She isn't sure what he means. "Please. Come in."

Inside the flat, Bill seems even bigger. He looms over her as she takes his wine and flowers and the space seems to shrink and feel cramped. She offers to hang up his jacket but struggles with the weight. He takes it from her.

"It's these." He pulls out a huge metallic cluster of keys and a padlock and chain placing them on the tablecloth. "From

TYNESIDE TALES

Rosewood." He smiles sheepishly. Natalya nods, remembering his day job at the school, and moves them to a cabinet.

Bill talks quickly. "They got a new gate on today. Magnetised. The headmistress doesn't like it but…"

Natalya suggests they have wine.

"Maybe I should have got vodka." Bill fiddles with one of the paper coasters she picked up free in town.

"Wine is fine." She smiles at her rhyme and savours the rich smokiness from the open neck of the bottle.

"Do you leave that open a lot?" Bill frowns at the balcony door.

"Sorry – are you cold?" Natalya moves to close it.

"It's just a bad signal. To intruders."

Natalya gives him his wine. "Cheers!" She lifts her glass.

"I don't suppose it's alarmed either."

Natalya shrugs. "It's nice to have some air."

"Ah but, you don't know who's watching." Bill takes a cautious sip. He frowns. "Is this all right?"

Natalya says "yes" and Bill admits he doesn't drink much wine, never buys it either.

"It's great," Natalya tells him, truthfully.

Bill nods, reassured, and tentatively drinks some more.

He isn't a handsome man, Natalya thinks, but warm and capable. He has good hair for his age. He even has hair on his fingers. So different from Pavel. She serves up the borscht.

"My dad grew beetroot on his allotment."

"Allotment?" Natalya asks.

"A little bit of land for vegetables."

"Oh good!" Natalya smiles. Everything seems bright and happy. Red wine, borscht and a man to eat it with. She tears some bread. "It's good to grow things, dig into the earth." Her cheeks feel flushed. She's alive.

"It got contaminated."

Natalya shakes her head at the word.

"Poisoned," Bill explains. "The council put ash on it."

Natalya frowns, she must have misheard.

"The council? They poisoned it?"

"Well, they didn't realise at the time."

Natalya shakes her head. Bill nods grimly.

"Aye, you've got to watch them. Have you tested your smoke alarm?"

Natalya says "no". Bill tells her that four out of five alarms are defective and she should burn some toast to see.

"I don't like smoke," she says.

"It's better to be safe than sorry."

"Better safe than sorry," she repeats.

"Yes, a very good saying that."

Natalya gets up from the table. She feels giddy and hot. Perhaps she should drink some water. She's drinking too fast. She fills a glass from the tap.

"Would you like some music?" It's too early but she's said it now.

"What you got?" Bill looks expectant.

"Oh. Just the radio." Natalya feels foolish. Her hand hovers over the dial.

"Aye, gan on. Why not?"

A jazzy baritone croons immediately. It's perfect. She begins to serve the dumplings, dousing them in stew. The warm aroma fills the air, envelops both of them.

"Lovely!" Bill exclaims as Natalya puts down his plate.

They eat, drink and listen. Natalya feels the juices of life play into her bones. She wants to dance, to sway under Bill's big shadow, invite his hands to her body.

"Gorgeous!" he slurps mid-mouthful.

The song on the radio ends and the announcer introduces the news. Natalya's arms tense. She places her cutlery on her plate and gets up quickly.

Bill looks alert. "Listen!"

Natalya turns the dial swiftly and words are swamped in hiss.

"What's the marrer?" Bill watches her.

She finds some music. Light and brisk, not as good as before.

"I prefer music." She sits down again.

"I thought with it being in Russia..."

"Yes." Natalya picks up her knife and fork.

"Would they have dogs?"

Natalya looks up at him.

"At the school, the caretakers, do they have dogs in Russia?"

"I – don't know." Natalya tells him honestly.

"Could have made a difference. Alsatians at the entrance. S'what I've been saying down at Rosewood. Nobody would mess with a dog."

Natalya feels frozen.

Bill leans forward. "People think it cannit happen. But looka." He points with his fork at the radio.

Natalya drinks the rest of her wine. She reaches for the bottle.

"They think I'm just the caretaker, but I've got volunteer experience." He pulls out a crumpled leaflet. Natalya reads the words. 'Neighbourhood Vigilance.' Bill points out the last sentence. 'We crack down on crime.'

She rises to clear the plates. Bill puts his hand on her arm.

"Sorry. I'll finish it." He scoops up meat on his fork.

Natalya carries her own plate to the sink.

He opens out a hand. "Firm but fair. And prepared."

Natalya drains her glass.

"I mean how'd they get in there, eh? Not enough security." His finger stabs down at the table.

Natalya shifts in her chair. He beams.

"That was lovely."

She blinks as if just waking up.

"Would you like some apple pie?"

Bill slaps his belly.

"Oh hey! Mebbies in a bit!"

Natalya's face feels tight. She twists at the stem of her glass.

"Least they've got the army there."

Natalya looks up at his smiling face.

"The Russian Army, eh?" he nods at her.

Natalya clears the rest of the table. Bill drums his fingers in time to what sounds like a military band. Natalya looks through the window at the crisp black night, her sad round face floating over the darkened land full of bright yellow lights.

She remembers the envelope. A white oblong on the table. Pavel, so neat and precise, even with a surprise.

"Open it."

She pulled out the theatre tickets. Two seats in the stalls. Not cheap, even in the Moscow suburbs. She read the name of the show, a musical.

North East.

But when the date came around, they'd argued. Pavel went alone.

As soon as she heard he was captive, she knew he'd never come back. She knew he wouldn't be one of those who would make a dash for it, recklessly risking a bullet. She knew he wouldn't even complain but would sit correctly in his seat, waiting to hear what to do.

She stood with others later, for hours, smoking in the rain, staring at the nondescript building. Children and pregnant women were freed unharmed. When the army arrived, Natalya was ushered away. A young policeman, his nails bitten down to the quick, took her name and politely drove her home. She was quietly shocked later to realise that, when it came to it, she too was obedient. She wanted to trust in authority, in her country, in reliable armed control.

Bill is standing next to her. "Are you all right?"

She nods automatically.

"It's a worry, eh?"

Natalya looks blank.

"Come on, lets see what…" He turns the dial on the radio.

A voice speaks in Russian. Gunfire is heard in the background. Natalya puts her hand to her mouth.

"Christ!" Bill pushes a hand through his hair. "Have you got a telly?"

Natalya holds her breath but Bill has turned already and opened her living room door. The sofa lit by two little lamps, ready for seduction. Bill blunders over and manhandles her TV. He stands pointing the remote control and finds the evening news. From the doorway, Natalya sees a flash of an ordinary school caught in a hail of bullets.

"Jesus!" Bill shouts, sitting sharply on the sofa's edge. "We need armed guards," he mutters.

Natalya stands at the door.

The picture changes, different news. Natalya walks slowly into the room. She wants to draw the curtains, turn it off, at least turn down the sound. She takes the remote control, softly clicks the button. The screen goes blank again.

"I'm sorry, I'm tired now."

Bill's mouth moves, bewildered. His eyes flick round for clues.

"I think I need to rest."

Alone in bed, between her new sheets, Natalya stares at the soft white square of the ceiling. She kept her ticket for *North East*. Seat 16, row M of the stalls. It would have been near the back, probably under the circle, where Pavel fell asleep.

Faith's Tale

Rachael Forsyth

Well the first time I saw her,
well I thought I didn't know her,
but I'm sure I'd seen her face before,
I couldn't think of where,
her blue eyes met mine in passing,
up the High Street in the morning,
and her look was so entrancing,
that me heart was mine nee mair.

A traditional Tyneside folksong

"**H**urry up. I want to get home some time today!"

Well if you didn't shove I wouldn't have to worry about falling down the gap beneath the train! I don't care about being run over by a train, just not while I'm wearing my new shoes.

"Move down the carriage will ya? Some of us are gonna get trapped in the bloody door."

If I could move I'd be ecstatic, at the moment I'd be content being able to breathe.

The shrill beep drilled into the weary minds of the travellers. Another day was ending and the drudgery of living in a major city was still tumbling along like the slow currents of the Tyne itself.

As the train rocked Amanda allowed her mind to wander; being so tightly packed into the carriage didn't allow her any other luxury. She tried to ignore the woman who talked loudly into her ear as she spoke to her colleague. Neither did she acknowledge each time the man behind her banged her arse with his copy of the *Financial Times*. If that lechy guy tries to peer down my shirt one more time, I swear I'll swing for him, she thought. Okay, she admitted to herself, maybe it was wearing these shirts that got me the job anyway, but that's beside the point. It had taken two years of savings and three years of confidence building before she finally moved out of home to face the burden of living alone in the city. Now, three months later, she was beginning to have second thoughts.

The chirruping phone was tossed aside as Amanda sank back into the leather beanbag and kicked her stilettos off. It was good to be home. Pouring the warm wine into the used glass she sighed and tried to ignore the insistent whine of her mobile. With a few gulps the wine was finished and Amanda sank deeper into the seat. A migraine began to pulse at the back of her eyelids, but still the phone kept on ringing. With more effort than was needed Amanda crawled over to the vibrating devil and barked a greeting to the caller.

"Good evening Miss Turner. This is Barclaycard calling, I was wondering if I could have a few moments of your time to tell you about an exciting new offer we have?"

"No you may not! Sod off!" Amanda threw the mobile down and collected together last night's dishes. She piled them into the sink, promising herself that she would wash them in the morning, but knowing she wouldn't. When the microwave pinged and a new bottle of wine was opened Amanda flopped back onto the sofa and aimlessly flicked through the TV channels. Summer's clemency was beginning to fail, but she didn't mind the chill that seeped through the open widow and through the thin fabric of her clothes. She stroked the lapel of her jacket lightly and smiled at the touch, but it was soon followed by a frown as she remembered the price tag. It had only taken two months for her to blow her entire savings. She was now living in a flat looking over the city lights that she could no longer afford and wearing clothes she couldn't dream of paying off. She drowned her sorrows in another glass of wine before smiling as something hopped into her lap. "I thought it was London that was meant to be the loneliest city in the world?" Absent-mindedly she stroked Charlie's ears as he nibbled the food, forgotten on her lap. "Didn't think I'd be in debt, with only a rabbit for company," she said bitterly as she emptied the bottle into her glass.

A job is a job, especially if it's a well-paid job. This was the new philosophy Amanda had adopted rather quickly. In such a short space of time she had waited tables, worked behind a bar, handed out leaflets (rather embarrassingly dressed, but that's best forgotten) before she landed a job with a large designer company that had recently opened on the outskirts of the city. True, she only got the job because she hadn't noticed that the new shirt she had bought especially for the interview bared more than she would have liked. But at least now she had a 'real' job, working hard between eight and five at night with an hour's battle travelling to and from work on the Metro. The thrill of the bright city had faded fast – grime and sweat is hard to romanticise after a hard day at work. Loneliness seemed to stalk the streets infecting people to the core. Amanda sighed as she sipped her third latte of the day. The only time anyone talks to me is when they want something, she thought. Today had been no exception. The fashion house she worked for bustled with activity, but none in her direction. Every morning the working fairies placed a large pile of documents to be typed, checked or filed and every evening they magically disappeared. It wasn't what she had in mind for her aspiring career in the fashion industry. Here she was wearing other people's designs when her own lay forgotten in a box she still hadn't got round to unpacking.

This day was different. Today she wore the same feminine, yet powerful suit but a long silver chain hung from her neck. The silver twisting pendant had been her first design and her first creation. Amanda strolled around in the office in her ridiculously high heels and with her glasses perched on the end of her nose. She could see better without them obscuring her vision to be truthful, but they looked good. Dark tresses framed her pale skin and she tried her best to pout and look secretively creative and genius-like, as they do in the films. But it did no good. No one so much as glanced her way, never mind saw the potential in the elegant pendant that had taken her weeks to carefully create. Utterly dejected Amanda stumbled out of the office and walked down towards her favourite delicatessen. True, it had taken her months to slim down to a size eight, but she knew the emotional comfort of the pastries that gleamed from behind the counter.

Ignoring the catcalls as she passed the building site, which never seemed completed, Amanda greedily tucked into the second Danish. Wearily she trudged toward the station, wanting to go home and yet not eager to face the emptiness of the flat. As she stepped onto the platform Amanda swore loudly as the station was still heavily packed. People pushed and bustled past her to find sanctuary on the narrow platform. A unified sigh echoed around the station as the train slowly pulled up to a stop. Thankfully, like the Tardis, there was enough room for everyone to cram into the small carriages. Amazingly, Amanda found herself trapped between a woman who was talking loudly to her colleague and, once again, the man behind her who managed to keep brushing her arse with his *Financial Times*. Amanda was about to say to herself that at least there wasn't a lechy old man staring at her boobs when she saw him. True, he wasn't old, but he was still staring at her chest as if he'd never seen a pair before. The overcrowded rumbling of the train grated her temper and out of the corner of her eye she saw the man continually stare at her. Long, brown locks hid most of his face so Amanda couldn't see who was taking such an interest. The train finally stopped between stations and the temperature rose. Further down the carriage a small child started to wail, the sound irritating all passengers. As the train sat waiting to pull into the next platform Amanda's patience snapped. The man's attention to her chest hadn't wavered; even though she had, infuriated, tried to move herself out of his line of sight, he merely followed her. Another child joined in the melodic wailing and the camel's back broke. Fuming, she turned to the man and snapped at him. "Hey buster, if you want to see a pair of tits so badly why don't you buy FHM like everyone else?" Sound evaporated from the carriage and all eyes turned to the sound of her voice. She didn't care whether she made a spectacle of herself or not; she was pissed off. The young man's face flushed with embarrassment and for the first time he looked up to her face. It was Amanda's turn to be taken aback. Behind the greasy locks of hair that obscured his face was a pair of the brightest eyes she had ever seen. Even in the dim glow of the tube lighting they dazzled with an ethereal light and shone a shade of blue that designers dream of. The man mumbled an apology and turned his gaze away from her, breaking the spell. Amanda blushed crimson, but thankfully the moment was lost as the train started once more and they pulled into the platform. The young man quickly stepped out onto the platform and Amanda sighed with relief. Sitting down she glanced out of the window as the train pulled out of the station and she was taken aback once more. The young man was standing watching her, his blue eyes staring at her as she left.

Another of Sod's Laws is that, when you're running late, you can guarantee that the transport links will be late as well. But Amanda wasn't even that lucky. After barely sleeping she was tired, grouchy and to top it all off the Metro was hardly running at all. So, after being crammed into a bus, she wasn't very happy to say the least. The scolding from a boss who, she realised, didn't even know her name, didn't help matters. But despite this she couldn't stop a smile from touching her lips. The young man's eyes had haunted her on the way home and through the night. Her resolve had broken in the small hours of the morning and she had spent the final hours working by the light of dawn. She had carefully wrought a pendant from silver sterling wire and placed delicately in the centre an azure stone that was a poor imitation of the colour of his eyes. The day passed painfully slowly but she was rewarded when it finally ended and she made her way home. The Metro was running normally and Amanda was pleased to get a seat on the train. Her heart dropped when she saw that the young man wasn't there. Why should he be, she scolded herself, and, dejected, she allowed herself to doze in between the few stops she had until she was home.

Fate often has other plans. Stepping out of the carriage she instinctively apologised as she bumped into someone as she came out of the door. "I shouldn't apologise," she grumbled to herself, "it's only common courtesy to let people off the train first before you barge your way on." A hand touched her arm lightly and she spun round to face whoever had the audacity to touch her. Even though the doors were closing she could see who she had bumped into. A smile touched the young man's lips and once more his gaze was set upon her chest. Amanda instinctively put her hand to her bosom to block his view, but she realised that beneath the palm of her hand was the necklace she had made. As if to acknowledge this, the man looked up at her face, the strange smile flickering behind his eyes. It wasn't until the train had left that Amanda turned to make the short walk home. She couldn't see that she wore the same smile that the man had, nor did she notice that she clutched the pendant as she walked home.

It is often the small things that make the biggest changes. Within a week Amanda had moved out of the expensive high-rise flat and was beginning to settle with Charlie in a smaller, but homely flat. Charlie settled quickly into the new surroundings and soon began to nibble the new furniture. Amanda had not seen the young man again, as much as her heart wanted to. She saw his eyes wherever she went, but she was just fooling herself. Loneliness had become a familiar friend, but one who now resorted to hanging around in the background – waiting to be acknowledged. Amanda now longed for the evenings as it was a time when she could focus on her work, both designing and creating the jewellery that had begun to plague her dreams. Work was less of a hassle as she had something to look forward to greeting her when she stepped back into the flat. It became even less of a hassle as she calmly handed in her notice of resignation. She felt none of the excitement and dread of branching out on her own; she could only feel calm. It had been months since she had met the young man on two brief occasions, but it had been enough to remind her why she was there and what her heart longed to do. The last day in the office passed as the first and any other had. No one noticed her departure; not that she expected them to. With the few effects she had littered on her desk tucked safely under her arm she stepped onto the train and sat in the packed carriage waiting for the last journey home.

Fate plays its games with us, as the wind will play with the leaves. Amanda had been so wrapped up in savouring the moment of not having to travel in the rush hour any more that she had not noticed who had been travelling in the same carriage. Nor did she notice what he slipped into the box on her knee. Now Amanda sat and toyed with the small velvet bag, its contents glittering on the table. A small business card had fallen from the bag first. All it said was 'Heaven' written in delicate blue script, but this didn't provide the most mystery. The black bag also contained two other items, a small silver angel figurine and a plastic compass. "What on earth are these for, Charlie?" Amanda didn't dare speak above a whisper. Her heart raced as she hoped she knew who had left them. "We have an angel. Okay, that's simple enough, but why a compass?" As she drained her glass of wine Charlie hopped onto the low coffee table, letting wafts of white hair fall to the carpet. He nibbled lightly at the compass, but finding plastic not to his taste he spat it from his mouth and began to chew on an apple from the fruit bowl. "Well thanks, some help you are." Amanda picked up the compass from the table and wiped rabbit-drool from the cover. "That's odd Charlie. I think it's broken. The arrow doesn't move, it's fixed on north."

It had never taken much to stir her curiosity but when it did Amanda was unable to resist. Summer had turned and autumn was beginning to take bites out of the climate. A bitter wind rose and fell like the tides, filtering through gaps in fabrics and chilling bare skin. Amanda shuddered as she stepped out of the car and she wound the scarf tighter round her neck. The sun glistened, but its heat was lost. Her hair whipped behind her as she slowly stepped across the grass. Beads of dew glistened on the ground and trickled through the gaps in her sandals. You picked a fine day to be fashionable, Amanda thought, but she could hardly hear her own voice. The thrum of the traffic engulfed her, its sound cocooning around her in a cacophony of noise. But, even surrounded by such a violent clash between the beauty of the world and the harshness of industry, Amanda failed to notice anything around her. Her gaze was set upon the giant figure that loomed overhead. It had to be here. The Angel of the North.

Silently she stepped towards the figure and placed a hand lightly on the metal frame. "Hello again." It had been years since she had been brought here but still she felt the awe of the dream and work that had been needed to create such an angel. Out of the corner of her eye she saw another velvet bag and quickly she opened the pouch. A small necklace slid into her open palm. The blue was perfect, the silver work was clumsy, but it was the stone in the centre that would make anyone part with their cash. It took her a moment to recognise the pendant but she was taken aback when she realised the necklace was an imitation of her own. Before her anger could flair a hand touched her arm gently. The brilliance of the man's eyes stunned her into silence as he passed a card to her. 'Heaven – designer jewellery by Amanda Turner'.

Sometimes cities can be the loneliest places in the world. Sometimes they're not soulless places, but rather they are soul-searching places. It just takes time to find what you're looking for. If you stand clear of the gap, how can you take that leap of faith?

TYNESIDE TALES

The
Homeleaver's Tale

Matt Forrester-Shaw

The best of men cannot suspend their fate.

Daniel Defoe

It was just an ordinary day when I decided that I could not live with my parents any more. Oddly enough, they were divorced, but still living in separate parts of the house. I was sick of the arguing, and of being told that my father had plans for me, while my mother was waiting for me to meet a nice girl and settle down. The woman can't take a hint. I'm twenty-two and she has never seen me with a girl. Mother said I was a late bloomer. As far as I was concerned, I didn't want to bloom, I was happy as a bud. I think father had his suspicions though. He had seen me around with my friends. When he had asked for help on the car, my mate Brandon had looked at him like he was being asked to build a lighthouse on the M1. I get the feeling that he realised we weren't going to be opening the batting for his team.

Father was a real man's man. He was involved with the local football club. If he wasn't down at the football club he would be working on some old wreck of a car in the garage. This was defiantly not my scene. I preferred the bright lights and dark recesses of the city. There was nothing I liked more than going for a drink, meeting some cutie guy and spending the night. Mind you, though, there were plenty of times when I went with a cute guy and woke up with someone that looked like they had been hit by a bus that had backed up to finish the job.

I remembered as a kid being taken to the football club and father being in the changing rooms with the team, who made jokes about 'dirty puffs' and other such things. Of course I had no idea what it meant at the time, but father joined in with what the other guys had been saying. There are still times when I wish I hadn't shown quite so much disdain for going to the football club. It drove the final wedge between father and me. Although, thinking about it, being in that changing room has kept me and my imagination amused on many a lonely night shut away in my closeted bedroom.

So, I'd decided to move, but where to? There were so many places that looked rather nice. I fancied something fairly central so I grabbed the *Evening Chronicle* father brought home each night and I started to read. Okay, something central was out unless my parents dropped dead in the night leaving me the house and a small fortune. Unlikely to happen, but you never know. So I looked a bit further out of town; nothing much there, either. How the hell was I supposed to fly the nest and make my way in the city if I couldn't even afford to live further away from the city, never mind somewhere actually in the city? Deciding that the only thing for it was to get my parents onto a plane being piloted by a suicidal orang-utan, I elected to sleep on it. With any luck, inspiration would take me roughly from behind during the night. Let's face it – living at home, nothing else was going to take me roughly from behind in the night.

Dawn broke the next day and I was awakened from my slumber by the warm rays of the early morning sun filtering into my bedroom and the yelling of my parents downstairs. I hopped up out of bed like a gazelle, took one look at the clock and hopped straight back in again. It was half six in the morning, and it was a Saturday. Burying my head under my pillow, I hid from my parents' row.

Later, at a more respectable Saturday time of nine o'clock, I awoke again. This was more like it. There were still voices coming from the kitchen as I donned my silk, Chinese print robe and headed down the stairs. As I entered the kitchen a mug whizzed past my head. Ah, I thought, they haven't made up yet. With that, a slice of toast came racing towards me, jam side heading for my right shoulder. I stepped smartly to the right and it hit me in the left shoulder. This was going to be a stain that would be a bugger to get out. I turned, catching a glimpse of myself in the mirror. I looked like a refugee from Abba sporting a toast broach. With that it was back upstairs to change, and dump the robe in the washing for mother to discover later.

Avoiding my parents as I left the house, I went to meet Brandon. We had been at school together in Sunderland and his brother had moved into Newcastle a few years ago. If anyone was going to know what to do, it would be him. Meeting Brandon on a street corner, I asked, "Had much business today?"

His only reply was to blow a raspberry. Blowing one back, I realised we were masters of a dying art. No one blew a raspberry any more, they just swore and gestured at each other.

Unfortunately, Brandon was unable to help. Apparently, his brother had bought the keys to a council flat off the best friend of his ex-girlfriend's sister's aunt who now lived in a penthouse after inventing underwire Y-fronts. Or something like that. My quest for every young adult's holy grail of leaving home now seemed further away than ever. Suddenly I was struck by inspiration – and by a sweet wrapper someone had chucked off the top deck of a passing bus. I would get a residential job in a bar. Frankie, my ex, or rather my Y (as in 'WHY did I sleep with you?'), could help. He knew some guys who owned just such a venue. Brandon decided to do the same and we both headed home to borrow money so we could catch a train to Newcastle.

The train arrived. It was one of those special trains that rail companies use on the hottest days of the year. All the windows were jammed shut and people with chronic body odour were scattered throughout the carriage in a way that left no option but to sit near one. Of course the train was late. After half an hour, we took a vote and agreed that this must be a new mobile sauna, and started looking for the lockers and towels. We arrived in Newcastle feeling like two overcooked cabbage leaves. Still, never mind, just a few streets behind the bustle of the station there was a wonderful little gentlemen's social club called Grand Central.

Brandon and I navigated to Grand Central, managing to avoid the beggars bumming fags from passers-by. We entered the bar and were greeted by Danny, another one of my Ys. Oh God, I thought to myself. It's 'This is your sex life!'.

"Well, well, well, what brings *you* here, big boy?" Danny asked in his lisping, insipid tones.

"Looking for a job, Danny," I replied. "This is my mate Brandon."

"Well, you're a fine young thing aren't you?" Danny said, looking Brandon over in an almost Dickensian way.

Brandon was not as savvy with the scene as I was. Being blond with a boy-band look had driven him into exile from the scene, hence avoiding all the leering and commenting which I also received but absolutely loved. Brandon blushed, replying in a small voice I had never heard him use before, "Err, thanks."

I grabbed Danny's attention back, "Frankie said we should come and have a chat with Mark about jobs."

"Mark? Which Mark?" Danny asked, without breaking his gaze at Brandon.

"Mark who owns this place," I said sharply.

Danny turned his attention to me. "Ohhh, you mean Mona." He went over to an intercom and said "Mona, there are two bits of trade down here for you." Crackling, the reply came "Okay dear, send them up to my room."

Uh-oh, I thought. Is this going to be a casting couch interview? Danny directed Brandon and me upstairs to the top room. Mark, the owner of the venue, was sitting on one of the club-style couches arranged around a low coffee table. He was wearing tennis shorts and top that looked about a size too small. There was a bar in the corner and the whole place had the feel of a chill-out area. Brandon and I sat opposite Mark, who uncrossed his legs. I felt Brandon give me a slight kick. I lowered my gaze slightly and saw why Mark had moved his legs. Staring right back at me was the last chicken in the shop.

"Right boys, what are you looking for?" Mark was talking to us.

"We're after jobs, residential jobs, sir," piped up Brandon, slightly too quickly.

"Well then, what can you do for me?" Mark asked. Brandon and I exchanged glances. Standing up stiffly, Mark then said, "Sorry, I can't sit like that for long. I had surgery yesterday."

"Oh, what did you have done?" I asked.

"I treated myself to lipo and a bit of an enhancement," said Mark, putting his hand on his waist then down to his groin.

"Really?" I said, "It doesn't show."

Mark looked speechless. Apparently, I'd not given him the response he wanted. I could feel Brandon trying to choke back laughter as Mark replied, "Hmmm. You're just the sort of mouth I want behind the bar. I've only got one job going at the moment. If you both want to split the work then you can, but you'll have to share the room next door."

We were taken by Mark to the room, which was really large and easily big enough for Brandon and me.

"Right then, I'll give you a day to think about it. Give me a call tomorrow and we'll make arrangements." He gave us his card.

Brandon and I positively rushed down the stairs. Saying goodbye to Danny, we went into the street bouncing with excitement.

"We gonna take it?" asked Brandon.

"Too bloody right we're going to," I said. "If we share the shifts then I can keep my day job as well."

"Fine with me," Brandon replied. "I'll do most of the shifts there then and we can share the room."

With that agreed, we both headed back to Central Station, and home to plan our move out of Sunderland, out of Suburbia.

On arriving home, I found mother in the garden, digging what looked like father's grave. On asking her what she was up to, I was informed that everyone had a wildlife pond these days. Seize the moment, I thought to myself, and told her that I was going to move out the next weekend. Mother was her usual stoic self and told me to sod off if I wasn't going to help.

When the time came, the drive into Newcastle was pretty uneventful. Brandon's father had already taken him down early that morning. Arriving outside Grand Central, I could see a slightly odd look on father's face. I got out of the car and heading towards me was Danny. Fabulous, I thought to myself. If father doesn't know what sort of people frequent here, he will as soon as Danny opens his mouth. Danny came marching smartly up, took father's hand and shook it firmly, saying,

"Thanks for bringing him down. I hoped he'd help us out tonight as we are a man down." I was flabbergasted. Danny had not spoken in his usual queeny tones but with a really deep, butch voice that didn't sound false.

Father followed Danny through to the bar, accepting the offer of a drink. I looked at father closely. Why wasn't he leaving? Surely he could see what kind of place this was – not *his* kind of place. Brandon and I unloaded the car taking the boxes into our room.

We worked quickly, going down to the bar after stuffing the last unpacked box in a cupboard. I saw father having a second drink. This was not good. I didn't want him hanging around and reminded him the car was on a double yellow line. He took a few more swigs of his drink and left. I asked Danny what they had been chatting about. "Nothing much," Danny said. He added that tonight, I was going to be working on the coat check for the club downstairs and Brandon was going to be taking money on the door.

The club opened at ten that evening and some people filtered down from the cabaret bar above. Brandon, his shirt wide open, was happily chatting away with, or rather, chatting up the bouncer. My first customer stopped to check a little bag and his T-shirt. He'd had his nipples pierced and there was a heavy chain linking them. "Want to pull my chain?" he asked.

"Why, will you flush?" I replied.

As the night went on, most of the guys handed over their tops and even some jeans, which kept me busy. Mona had wanted my sharp wit and I could see why now. It was like some kind of sport. Guys passing would make a comment, and I would make one back. Tit for tat.

At last I got a break and the chance to look around. Two guys were lip-wrestling near the bottom of the stairs. They stopped and carried on down the steps, pulling their T-shirts over their heads. I said, "Well. I was wondering if you two were going to give me the full show."

"Why? Would you want one?" came the reply, in an all too familiar voice.

There standing before me in outfits with more leather than a furniture factory, were Danny and my father.

An Angel's Tale

Dorothy Milne

Dance te yer Daddy, maa bonny laddy

Dance te yer Daddy, te yer Mammy sing

Ye shall have a fishy, on a little dishy

Ye shall have a fishy

When the boat comes in.

William Watson

Or should it have been, 'If the boat comes in'? The day had started well; my father had left at around four in the morning. Off fishing on a Saturday, a routine that I remembered from the moment I could walk. My mother had always sung that song to me from an early age. Of course, now I was far too mature at the ripe old age of fourteen, which might not sound very old, but little did I know of the fate that awaited my untarnished, unblemished and intact existence and the adventure I would embark on, which would result in evolving from boy to man.

I'd travelled on the Metro from Tynemouth to Newcastle, usually a very enjoyable journey but today it was quite different. My mother, I sensed, was rather agitated and I knew why. We'd called in at my grandmother's on the way to the station. Now my mother, who always dressed rather casually, was wearing a skirt. This was a rare occurrence and I soon realised that it would be an even rarer occurrence thanks to my grandmother, who was and always had been quite a feisty lady. She was often blunt and didn't suffer fools lightly.

"Oh you've got a skirt on! That makes a change; I must say you do look better in trousers. I always said you had footballer's legs, just like your father's." I couldn't believe what I was hearing; my smirk was quickly ousted by a very straight face as my mother glared at me.

"Come on, we're going." With that, I was dragged out of the house by the arm. The journey to Newcastle had been largely silent; I'd tried to speak a few times and made matters worse by saying that I wouldn't mind if someone had said that to me.

"Well, Alex, this may surprise you, but for a woman to hear that she's got footballer's legs is no compliment, I can assure you!" I suppose, me being rather naive, I didn't fully appreciate the severity of the verbal assault, but hey, I thought, wasn't that what mothers were for, speaking the truth, and wasn't it their duty to insult? Beneficial and positive criticism they liked to call it. The sunlight was beaming into the carriage and then flickering as we passed various trees and buildings. I studied my mother's facial expressions intently; every flash of light illuminated her face, which looked progressively angrier each time I looked. I decided quite quickly that it wasn't worth attempting polite conversation.

We arrived in Newcastle city centre around eleven and, as usual, the atmosphere was buzzing. We ascended the stairs out of the Monument Metro station and, as always, my mother commented on how elegant the buildings on Grey Street looked.

"They don't build them like that any more," she said. My age didn't allow me to appreciate fine architecture. I was more relieved to realise that my mother's mood had softened. Those 'footballer's legs' comments would, I suspected, take a while to forget and I concluded that this was the last day her legs would be exposed to the sun for the foreseeable future. We were meeting my mother's friend Fay for lunch; we headed towards Chinatown where we were going to try out the new restaurant in preparation for my father's birthday. On the way we passed an internet cafe and I thought of my beloved computer and how it would have to manage an afternoon without me. We entered the restaurant and immediately saw Fay beckoning frantically to come over to the table.

"You'll never guess what happened to me on the way in," she didn't give us a chance to speak. "I was driving along on the western bypass and I glanced upwards and to the right to gaze at the Angel of the North, which I always do, and you're not going to believe this, but he wasn't there!"

"Oh come on, that's ridiculous, he can't just vanish," my

mother replied. "You must have been mistaken. Maybe the light had played a trick on you, or maybe you'd glanced up at the wrong point."

"I know what I saw, or rather what I didn't see. Anyway I was parking up and about to turn off the radio when a newsflash came on. It said that a number of listeners had rung in to report the disappearance of the Angel of the North. We can't all be mistaken, can we?" I smirked; I didn't believe a word of it. Fay had always been a bit eccentric. But then the radio reports, how could you explain that? I convinced myself that it must have been a ludicrous hoax and as for Fay, well, she must have been mistaken. The meal was delicious and before we knew it we were saying our goodbyes and heading home.

We arrived home around three and were slightly worried by my father's absence; he was always waiting for our return on a Saturday afternoon. We'd usually have a stroll around the harbour and later, if I wasn't out with friends, we'd watch DVDs and snack all night. My mother I knew felt pangs of guilt. They'd argued the night before. They hardly ever argued as a rule, but last night was different. I'd heard my father saying that fish stocks were dwindling and he would have to fish in a different area. My mother stated that she knew which area he meant; the locals called it the 'triangle of doom'. No one had fished there for years as it was considered too dangerous. A number of boats had gone down, there were very strong currents and the rocky areas were too numerous to mention. My father had said that it was just superstitious old wives' tales and the claims about the area being cursed were absurd and totally irrational. I'd listened to the ongoing argument in bed, covering my ears to try and block out the droning tones. Eventually I must have fallen asleep, as the next thing I'd heard was my father leaving for work.

My mother figured he might have gone to the Golden Lion, after selling the catch of the day, but that thought was cruelly dismissed when the phone rang. I watched bewildered as my mother let out an agonising groan and her legs buckled underneath her. It was Cathy, one of the crew members' wives. She told her that the three crew members were missing, the boat wasn't back in the harbour; they'd contacted the coastguard but there had been no mayday messages received. The lifeboat was launched, but there was nothing to be found, no boat, no crew; the weather could not have been calmer. The Met Office had issued no weather warnings, the boat was seaworthy; it was old, but well-maintained.

I knew that my mother didn't hold much hope of finding my father alive. Even though there had been no weather warnings, the North Sea could be treacherous and unpredictable. We hugged each other, something we hadn't done for a number of years, and we both sobbed uncontrollably. I eventually went up to my bedroom and lay on the bed. In my stomach I experienced the dullest ache that I'd ever felt. I could not fully grasp the intensity of the situation I had been plunged into, or the ongoing pain that I would have to endure of not knowing what had happened that morning. It was very harrowing to hear the sound of my mother's cries drifting up the stairs.

Later that night I heard the unlocking of the front door. I leaped off the bed and to the window, filled with false optimism. Could it be my father? Feelings of elation were immediately replaced with confusion as I saw it was my mother heading down the main street and towards the harbour. I grabbed a jacket, raced downstairs and locked the front door behind me. Where could she be going? I followed but stayed out of view. She arrived at the harbour walls and walked right along to the very edge, where the headland juts out. I watched as she suddenly stopped and stared out to sea. She was willing for my father's return, pining for him. It was heartbreaking to watch her lonely, desperate vigil. In silence she stood for what seemed like an eternity, then suddenly turned and headed towards home. As she passed the moonlight illuminated the look of desperation on her face. I wanted to follow her but strangely I was drawn to the ocean. I walked forward and watched in silence. The sea looked angry, grey raging waves crashing against the harbour walls. I was very bitter. How could you take my father, how dare you, I thought to myself. The ocean retaliated by launching even louder waves in my direction, as if it were ascertaining its power and authority against me, a mere mortal. The sea mist was swirling. There was an eerie atmosphere and a chill in the air; suddenly I went very cold. The mist was clearing out at sea and I could see what looked like a large figure appearing in the fog. I heard a quiet but deep voice, which seemed to be drifting over the ocean.

"Look in the rocks, the challenge you're faced with will become clear." As quickly as the vision had appeared it was hidden, obscured by the swirling sea mists. Drifting on the air came the haunting sound of a woman's voice, "Ye shall have a fishy, When the boat comes in". Had I imagined it? Of course I had, my mind was playing tricks on me.

The next morning I awoke, slowly then abruptly as I remembered about my father. I lay, slowly gathering my thoughts and realising that the dull ache in my stomach had returned. There was a knock at the door. I jumped out of bed and could see the police car outside. I feared the worst, when suddenly I heard my mother's voice.

"Alex, they're alive, they've been found!" I couldn't describe the feeling of immense elation, as I leaped downstairs shrieking. They had been found, minus the boat, washed ashore on rocks near St Edward's Bay. Strangely, their skin was found to be entirely coated in a coppery substance. They seemed to be lucid enough but when they began their tale, well it puzzled everyone. They'd been fishing as normal, near the forbidden area, but not within it. The seagulls were chasing the boat, waiting for scraps thrown overboard. Suddenly they'd gone quiet, then disappeared, but no sooner had they vanished than three appeared again flying closely together, a sign of impending doom in fisherman's terms. It was then that the bow of the boat seemed to crash against something and they were roughly tossed to and fro. The rudder shook furiously and they remembered being thrown violently overboard, entering the water, then a feeling of immense pleasure and serenity took over as they were scooped out of the water and onto the rocks. The strange story made headline news, not just in the North East but also around the globe.

It was three days later when it happened again, another boat had mysteriously vanished. This time the coastguard had picked up a mayday message, the location was pinpointed and the lifeboat was launched but there was nothing to be found. Ripples and froth were all that remained and there was an eerie silence hanging over the ocean. Two days passed and nothing, until a local man was walking along Prior's Haven when he spotted the entire fishing party. They, too, were glowing with that mysterious coppery dust and told the tale of feeling safe after entering the water and being lifted to safety. What was going on? After hearing the latest news I was reminded of that mysterious voice; my father was safe, that was all that mattered, wasn't it?

I headed down to the beach, mystified by the strange goings-on and feeling like I had a part to play in this unsolved mystery. I started walking along the beach and onto the rocks. What was I to look for? Suddenly out of the corner of my eye something seemed to be glistening in the sunlight. I reached down and saw a small bottle; it looked very old and had a strange lustrous sheen to it. There was something inside but I decided to wait until I got home to examine it. Carefully I released the cork and with the help of a pair of tweezers reached inside to reveal a small bit of parchment. I unrolled it and began to read.

A century ago I was never found
I've grown weary of my wife and son's haunting sound
Their mourning voices fill the air
All I ask is for you to care
I've put the sailors to the test
In the hope I'll finally be laid to rest.

I sat stunned. What was this enigma unfolding before my very eyes? I took the bottle and its contents to my history teacher, who lived in the next street. He was baffled and said he'd pass it on to the local historian. Two days later my history teacher rang. The historian had checked and double-checked the authenticity of the bottle and its contents; they were indeed old, probably from the turn of the century. He'd also studied old newspapers and thought he'd found the connection. The teacher went on to tell the story of three local fishermen who got into difficulty off the North East coast, on the second of July 1905, the same date as my father's boat went missing but exactly one hundred years ago. The boat was never found; two crew members were found washed ashore a week later but the third member of the crew was never found. Searching through subsequent newspapers the historian had discovered that the missing man's wife and son had hired a small boat and gone out to sea to lay flowers near the spot where the boat was last seen. The weather had started out all right but had quickly changed; they had both perished and were washed ashore a week later. The boy had been fourteen years old and my eyes widened when my teacher mentioned his name, Alexander James Monroe! The same as mine!

I headed back to the beach that afternoon. I couldn't take all of this in. The sea was very serene, the water a deep cobalt blue. I stood there staring, in a trance-like state. Suddenly I felt extremely cold, and I heard that same deep voice drifting over the ocean. "Lay him to rest, to break the curse, or the tragedy will continue."

I ran home. My father was there and I relayed all that I knew and realised what must be done. My father didn't believe a word of it. "Oh Alex, be rational, an operation to lift a boat that may or may not be there would cost thousands of pounds. Do you honestly think anyone in their right mind would believe you? All this nonsense about strange voices and that note in the bottle, it's probably a fake!"

"Well how do you explain the coppery substance on your skin? Look, it's still there!" My father looked down and had to admit that it wouldn't wash off. He also had difficulty explaining to himself how they had ended up safe on the rocks, but my reckoning didn't convince him. I was incensed, enraged and feeling very helpless in the desperate situation I was embroiled in. What more could I do?

That night, the worst storm in decades hit Tynemouth full-force. I could hear the rain lashing onto the windows and the ocean's raging waves crashing against the harbour walls. Thank goodness my father wasn't at sea tonight. I eventually drifted off to sleep. The next morning I heard lots of voices outside. I rushed to the window and saw everyone was heading to the beach. I woke my parents, quickly dressed and headed down to the shore. There, washed up on the sands, was a boat, an old boat by the look of it. The area was already being cordoned off but I managed to slip under the tape. There were two men on the boat and the police were keeping people back. I heard one of the men on board saying there was a skeleton in the hold. I stepped forward, reached out to the hull of the boat and slowly ran my fingers over the nameplate, clearing the sandy residue. I could just make out the name, 'Angel of the North'.

It was a late Sunday evening as the salvage vessel and boat made their sombre journey up the Tyne. The people of the North East had all followed this story very closely and they lined the banks of the Tyne; as a mark of respect they slowly bowed their heads as the vessels passed. They proceeded under the Millennium Bridge and as soon as they had passed underneath, the eye of the bridge closed and opened up immediately, faster than ever before, as though it were winking. The man operating the bridge controls watched in amazement. Suddenly all the lights in Tyneside went out and the aurora borealis came the furthest south it had ever been, glowing curtains of greenish yellow lights swirling to a magnificent merger across the skies.

Looking back, people realised that the passengers on the East Coast mainline weren't mistaken when they said that the Angel of the North had vanished at certain times in the past month. He had in fact saved the sailors, embracing them in his large rusty coloured wings in order to rescue his namesake and free the city from a century-old curse.

A Tall Tale

Peter Marshall

Like someone's love once dreamed about

But not possessed and longed for now

Sean O'Brien

It wasn't real love. I knew that. Deep down, at least, I knew it, but damn it felt good.

Selling insurance on the phone to people who didn't know what had hit them. BANG. One minute they might be serenely watching *Gardener's World* with a hot cuppa, the next I would have fixed them up with a hundred grand's worth of life cover that they didn't even need.

There's a knack to this selling business. It's cut-throat. You have got to want it, mean it, live it and yeah, you really have to love it too.

The feeling never lasted very long, but when it came, when you nailed the sale, oh boy, it was like nothing else. It made me feel alive. Look at me, look at me, LOOK AT ME! The big hotshot. The best seller on the team, that's what mattered. Attention on me and only me. The way the team leader looked at you when you sold another policy was what we all craved. When you are up in this game, they love ya. The problems start when you're down.

Newcastle had always intrigued me. The bright lights lured me in. It was as though they spoke to me, showing me the way. Coming from a small lump of coal for a village meant that Newcastle's sparkling diamond ways were practically alien to me, but I wanted to jump aboard the spaceship and fly.

As a child, the sights, smells and sounds (especially that irrepressible accent) in Newcastle stopped me in my tracks. I imagined leaving the small-minded mentality of country life and hitting the big smoke for years. A visit to the city would excite me for months. Although I pondered running away from home (at eight years old I even packed a small rucksack filled with crisps, an apple, a carton of juice and my favourite baggy jumper. I evidently felt that this survival kit would keep me going for months and that Newcastle's streets would keep me safe), it never quite happened. The furthest I ever got was my 'den' at the bottom of the garden. More languishing in the mud than lapping up the landmarks of lands unknown.

Now I am here. Living the proverbial dream, of sorts anyway. I made the move around six months ago. My mum cried. "Tell him Jim. Tell him he can't go. This is his home, it's where you belong. You're only nineteen and you won't be able to cope without me and your dad. I can't bear it Jim. Tell him. My youngest son flying the nest."

On and on it went. Sobbing, then screaming, then crying, weeping and laughing and shouting. But I had to go. I knew I didn't belong. Newcastle beckoned.

As you can see, my mother is somewhat of a worrier. The woman is also extremely protective of her children – five boys. The fact that all my brothers had moved out of the family home meant that my announcement to flee was hitting her hard. She looked after us well. Probably too well now I think about it actually, especially when I look in the mirror. At twenty-six stone I am not only the youngest, but also the lightest member of the Cooke family.

Cooke by name and cook by nature. God, could my mum cook. Steak, chips, pies, lasagne, spaghetti bolognese, trifle, Sunday lunch, jam roly-poly (got to be suet – beautiful stuff), sticky toffee pudding; the list goes on. The point is, it was damn good. The second point is, there was loads of it. The third point is, I filled my boots and now my boots are size sixteen.

Life in Newcastle was just what I wanted for a while. The excitement, wonder and magic that I had longed for, for all those years, was mine at last. I told myself to grab on tight and enjoy the ride. Which I did for a time. The problem was that I wanted to make the ride more exciting and kinda, well, sort of, started making things up.

There was one unexpected advantage of big city living. More people. Well, more importantly, more female people. The girls in Newcastle are wondrous creations. Feisty and fun in equal measure and always looking absolutely fantastic.

One problem remained, however – snaring one of these creatures was proving particularly difficult. That's when it started. I never really meant to do it, just once I did I couldn't stop. In my head the story seemed so right that I almost thought if I said it enough it would come true. You see, there was this particularly quiet girl at work, Helen, that to my mind was perfect marriage material. When she turned me down at the first hurdle (when I asked if she fancied a drink), the wedding was suddenly much further away. The asking of this question had also been quite hard. In fact, I had been goaded into it by a number of macho colleagues. So, when they asked how it went, I casually, without really thinking about it, just, made it up.

"Oh yes, no problem boys, check *me* out. You lads should take a leaf out of my book. How could she turn me down? We're off to the Dog for a drink tonight."

Lies, lies, lies, lies, lies! What was I doing? Why on earth did I say that? I am a fool. The thing is, once you have said something like that, you can't go back on it, not easily. So, these fantasy dates carried on. As far as the lads in the office were concerned, in a month, me and Helen had been to Venice, bought a house, got engaged. GOT ENGAGED?! What was I thinking? It was becoming more and more ridiculous and I couldn't stop. An engagement, however, usually requires a ring. When Helen came to work day after day without one, the game was up.

So, here I am. Where I want to be. Or so I thought back when I lived at home. I had made the jump from stifling small streets to stimulating city slickers. However, something just ain't quite right (that is, apart from the obvious ridicule since the Helen scandal). Something I can't quite put my finger on, it's…well, it's just not what I had expected and anticipated in all those daydreams.

TYNESIDE TALES

Okay, I'll be honest. I really saw Newcastle city as the stepping stone to something more, something magical. Hey, if that dancer bloke from Billy Elliot can make it, anyone can can't they? Including me. Next stop Hollywood, which, in turn, in my mind at least, would be the step toward superstar, world domination. You see, I had always had the gift of the gab, hence the job in telesales. This quality, coupled with my six foot four, twenty-six stone frame, had landed me the audacious role as the giant in the local amateur dramatic society's production of 'Jack and the Beanstalk' back home. The reviews had been more than generous:

A towering display from Cooke that forgives the minimal performance.
The District Herald

Needless to say, I took this as a great compliment and expected more 'towering display' opportunities to beckon in the capital. Yet so far, not even an opportunity of above average height had presented itself.

Work is starting to drag (which is made all the worse for the phantom engagement). It takes me an hour and a half to get there, despite only travelling roughly fifteen miles. Long gone are the good ol' days of riding my push-bike to work. Not being able to afford a place in the centre means that I spend half my day either having to make polite chitchat to a guy who just will not shut up or being dribbled on by a dozing commuter on the bus. It was only meant to be a stopgap until Quentin (Tarantino) got in touch.

Now, even the almighty high that I used to experience when selling seems to be diminishing with every sale. It is no longer cut-throat with a me, me, me attitude in a good way; more despicable, self-obsessed, ego-maniac behaviour in a seriously bad way, and it's starting to get to me down. Seriously down with a capital D. Down, down, deeper and down. The problems are starting. Sinking into the ground, it's almost like I am literally disappearing. My insides are hurting. Could it be my soul? The constant pressure of selling this insurance to little old ladies is killing me. Physically hurting me and emotionally damaging me. Could it be that my mum was right, that I can't cope without home? This vast metropolis that is the big smoke is too much. The streets are not paved with gold but are covered in smut and sweat of all who tread them.

Sod it. I'm through. I am heading home for one of mother's steak pies. Now that's REAL love.

A Fashionable Tale

James Macfarlane

What happens in the Koan Interview is private

and must never be repeated.

James Macfarlane

He was such an optimist, though in a flat like that it would have been difficult to hold a dark thought. He'd long forgotten his father until a line from one of his hippy songs came to haunt him, the trace of an earworm rhyming Tyne with all mine.

Perhaps it was the fifty-foot long living space of steel, maple and glass that inspired him, or the thought that she would like such things. Without the fog he might not have bought the place at all. It was perfect, he decided, except the bath would have to go to make way for the two metre Jay Kay Design spa in which they could both fit comfortably. When he told her about the bedroom she said there was no need for a four-poster but he liked the idea, as if their bed would be so much better than with two or three posts. It might have been the bright airiness of the room that drew him, light flooding in from a pale spring sun low above the fog. There was certainly a vision. His father had been a man of the old quayside, a fugitive down there. None of that mattered now, none of it was so real as his vision of their first breakfast together at the Lavarsi table with this view. It was like flying to look across the Tyne at the penthouse floors of the apartments opposite, the Sage squatting in Gateshead like a molten greenhouse and the Baltic arts centre sticking up through the fog.

The first morning he woke tired, struggling into local time with chores to be done before she arrived. He shaved then went into the living space and sniffed at a trace of last night's bachelor takeaway. He walked fifty feet to open the window, letting in frosty air to nip at every offensive odour then returning to set up his Pulita. He could never froth milk with the contraption but it looked good with its pipes exposed and a calibrated gauge on the gleaming pressure cylinder. He took his coffee black, wrapped his laundry in two pillowcases and set off down the hill.

Two pre-school children were using the laundrette as their

playground. He put his wash on and picked up a tattered celebrity magazine. He thumbed through it while an unshaven man sat with his head in his hands, apparently suffering. He looked more closely at the magazine a second time then left for something better.

Within a hundred yards he was in the 'rising area' the agent had described, more at ease among the gentrified boutiques and shops. He was looking for a decent hairdresser or a Café Che franchise when he saw the design gallery. It gaped like a pharmacological lab stripped of work except for three pieces sparkling under concealed lighting. On the right a shining porcelain mass after Henry Moore with bath taps and on the left a spindly frame after Alberto Giacometti, Don Quixote with a shower tap for a heart. In the middle was a stainless steel cube, one thousand millimetres each side. These three pieces were the shortlist of this year's 'Designs for Life'. The cube had won. In front of it a laser projection read, 'Kikan – answer your koan'.

Two hours later he put fresh water and coffee in his Pulita. He was waiting for the steam when she came in wearing her dressing gown.

"I thought you were bringing me a coffee?"

He shrugged and pointed at the Pulita.

"What are all those clothes doing here? Your shirts are everywhere. Darling we said we weren't going to let this place get like before."

"I didn't have time to finish the drying."

Work kept them away, from both each other and their home. Coming back after a week, his train stopped on the bridge as if to take in the sight of the flat. He had a surprise planned for her.

"Darling, I'm home," she called coming into the living space. "Wow, what's this?"

He told her what the design gallery curator had said. "Kikan is a difficult concept. Design as a work of art."

"But it's still a washing machine."

"No. It has that function but the form doesn't necessarily follow. It's a piece, a piece of art."

"It doesn't look like a washing machine."

"That's the idea. The form is not there. You don't go round thinking about washing all the time. But if you need it...Cool or what?"

"Where are the controls?"

"There are none. You tell it what to do."

"And it listens?"

"Controls cost money. This has an audio transducer. You programme it with your voice. If it's not sure it'll ask and you tell it until it recognises you. After that it has a record of your voice pattern. Commands are easy. And SS20 stainless steel. You could pour sulphuric acid on it. Beautiful isn't it?"

"Does it have to be so big?"

"It's the drum."

Before he could say more someone came to the door and she left.

The gallery had declined to perform installations but gave him a list from which he'd chosen a fitter over the phone. His fitter looked at the stainless steel cube with the dull eyes of one who drank most of their calories then walked to the window. Two units had been removed from the alcove to create space but the Kikan was ten centimetres higher than the counter. It wouldn't fit.

"Some view you've got here," said the fitter.

"Everybody says that."

They stood looking out over the bridges crossing and re-crossing between the shibboleth temples opposite.

"That's where I live," said the fitter pointing downriver to the thrifty streets and concrete hives below Byker where two gantry cranes swung above the last working dock. "There's a load of money comin' in here right enough."

"Look, what are you going to do about this?"

"If you really want it there you'll have to cut the granite in a workshop. If I was you I'd put it on the end."

"You mean out here in the living space?"

"It's up to you," said the fitter shifting on his feet, "I'm only here to do the fitting."

"But there is more work to do now than before I bought it. I'll call the gallery."

"You hired me. All they do is show. This'll cost me a day."

He was uncertain what to do and refused to pay anything until the job was done.

Returning two weeks later he looked towards the flat while re-crossing the bridge. His mind's eye could still see the maple floor scored and scraped where the kitchen units had been reset. It had taken four men to carry away the granite worktop. There was a deep gash where the slab had been dropped and dust clung to the B23 paintwork, degrading it to any old beige. With the sink out and the counter gone he would have to fill the kettle from the bath and boil it on the floor for instant coffee.

She needed a break. There had been so much to do, meeting caterers between dress fittings and fixing a seating plan that her matron of honour advised could never be laid out too soon.

"Darling," she greeted him at the door in her underwear, "I didn't think you'd notice."

Afterwards he opened a bottle of champagne and phoned the restaurant to postpone their booking. Their second coitus was long, slow and enduring, noisy for her and a late climax for him.

They finished the bottle before they left for the restaurant, a large-plates-small-portions place with no more than ten covers. After a piercing Sancerre with the langoustine, he wanted something more voluptuous for the main course and picked out a Hermitage black enough to fill his pen with. Back at the flat they came in exalting in the size of the living space, filling the place with music and waltzing playfully together until they banged drunkenly into the Kikan. He talked to it to make her laugh, shouted at it then kicked it, explaining that it was SS20 steel and he could pour sulphuric acid over it without harm.

"Come to bed," she said.

He let her go and shut off the music. It was silent. He went to the Kikan and listened. It was completely silent. He got down on all fours and put his ear to the floor in front of it. Still there was no sound. When he got to the bedroom she was already asleep.

Next morning he had a hangover bound tight with notions of guilt. When he reached for her she turned away. He got up for a glass of water and saw the Kikan, all form and function, the circle squared. There came a bizarre recollection of having shouted at it the night before. He went up to it and pushed the door. Nothing happened. Of course, even the door latch had servo operation. There must be a power problem. He looked into the service cupboard at the distribution panel and saw one of the circuit breaker switches out of line. Simple. He took a bar stool inside the cupboard, climbed on top and re-set the breaker. When he took the stool back into the living space and replaced it he heard a click from behind the cupboard door. The power supply had tripped again. He reset the breaker. It tripped again. He reset it three times.

"For God's sake do you have to make all that noise?"

He came from the window to put his arm round her, almost an achievement to cross a room the length of a sprint on his first school sports day. They stood together a while looking at the Kikan.

"Three thousand pounds," she said running her fingers along the edge of the piece.

"Why Kikan?"

"It's an answer to a koan."

After she had gone back to bed he took out the manual and skimmed through it several times, stopping at 'Troubleshooting', 'Turning On' and 'Programming'. An hour later he took a couple of aspirin, picked up his washing and set off for the laundrette.

A dog-owning vagrant had joined the children and the unshaven dipsomaniac enjoying the soap-scented heat in the laundrette. He loaded his wash and sat watching the machine, developing with each turn the conviction he'd been wronged. Since the problems were none of his making someone had to take the blame. They could continue indefinitely if he did not act.

His head was throbbing by the time he reached the gallery and the attendant did not recognise him. They kept him waiting a quarter of an hour before he saw their curator who then suggested the Kikan had been wrongly installed. Worse, his fitter had been making nuisance calls to the gallery complaining about payment.

"The fitting is none of our business," said the curator, "but as a valued client we'll send someone round to take a look."

While he was arguing with the design gallery the laundrette had locked up with his washing inside. He struggled through the following week with only three shirts.

On his return, the gallery was adamant that the problem was his.

"You used a thirteen amp circuit breaker for the piece," said their representative.

"That was the fitter," he told them, "I didn't wire it."

When he telephoned his fitter there was no answer. He left a message, clear but not courteous, blaming him for the wiring mistake and refusing to pay a penny. No matter what he did this weekend, the most he could achieve would be to find an electrician prepared to run new cables. He made his calls and went to recover his washing.

They stayed in that night and ordered a takeaway. After they had eaten they took a bath together, made love and lay across the Italian sofa watching television. She had long fine hair, auburn with natural highlights. He laughed once when, taking herself seriously during a visa application, she described the colour as red and blonde with a bit of dark brown through it. "Like the Belgian flag," he suggested and still teased her two years later.

It never occurred to him something so beautiful needed so much looking after until they lived together. Then he discovered she spent fifteen to twenty minutes each day just brushing it.

The television had a fault. The film they'd been watching seemed to cue an advert. Instead the screen faded to white and silence.

"There's still a signal," he said nodding at the screen. As he spoke the dull white, almost silver-grey seemed to be pink. Then it was orange. They watched it lighten through yellow, shifting through green-blue before brightening to pink again, repeating quickly again and again while a voice said, "What is the sound of one hand clapping?" The rainbow tints repeated in a blurr, blazing brilliant white as a voice said, "Kikan".

Late after midnight he came tumbling from a deep sleep to answer the phone. An emotional voice, a familiar voice, was calling him unpleasant names and otherwise not making sense. He thought it was his father saying, "I've done everything for you". He could not place the caller or his drunken ramblings until, "Give me my money or I'll bloody kill you.'" He put the phone down and tried to sleep.

In the mail he found a note written in blue biro with careful handwriting like that of a child. It read, "I done everything you asked. I need money desperately." He put the note on the Kikan and pressed the top right hand corner. A servo clicked and in a precise outward movement the door opened up a gap of five centimetres on either side before rotating. There was no spring, no catch, all smooth as oil.

After sorting through his laundry this time there was no going down on all fours. He didn't so much as incline his head to say, "Kikan. Wash my whites at forty degrees."

"White. What temperature please?"

"Forty," he said, pronouncing with more of an umlaut this time if not exactly an 'r'.

"Forty," the machine confirmed.

He loaded his washing, filled the powder tray and poured in a cap full of fabric conditioner. He called, "Go."

Nothing happened.

He called, "Wash." He called, "Go you stupid bloody thing."

Still there was no response.

He looked at the manual and said, "Kikan go," a faint click sounded and the dispenser drawer drew shut. The door swung then closed the last fifty millimetres in a parallel slide. He bent down to listen but could hear nothing. Another two hours later he had still heard nothing. When he pressed the door at the top right hand corner this time nothing happened. He dialled the design gallery, surprised that he knew the number by heart.

They put him on hold. Five long minutes later he hung up and called again. The curator was still unavailable but would return his call later.

"You say the fault is in the piece?" asked the curator.

"Definitely."

"How can you be so sure?"

"Because four hours ago I put the first wash in after three months and nothing has happened."

"What error code does it say?"

"There isn't one."

"That's serious."

He put the phone down and kicked the Kikan.

A gallery rep came round with a black box. The door opened when he pressed it. A little display on the box blinked four asterisks.

"There is no fault code. That means there is something wrong with the installation unless," he pressed another button. "See. Heat pump shut down. In an ordinary machine you don't have one but with this recycling all the energy it's incredibly efficient." He reached down to engage something underneath and pulled out the whole unit, scoring the floor with tiny pieces of grit. "It looks as if everything is in order. Wait a minute. Let me check." He ran the hot water until steam clouded round, then reached in the back. "Just as I thought. Hot and cold water are the wrong way round. It has to cut out or the heat pump explodes."

After the rep had gone he took the childish note from the top of the Kikan and tore it in little pieces.

While he was away she looked in the phonebook and called a fitter to change the installation. The red and blue tags marking hot and cold pipes were crossed. There was no other fault.

"Kikan," she called out. "Wash, white, cotton at sixty degrees."

"White. Sixty degrees." Her voice recognition engaged first

time. The dispenser drawer clicked shut and the door swung to. When he called her that night she sounded happy.

Two weeks later when his train stopped on the bridge he looked out over the fog, picking out their apartment on top of the hill. She was there ahead of him this weekend, busy with the last preparations for their wedding. He felt extraordinarily pleased until he passed the design gallery. Moore and Giacommetti had been replaced by cubes of stainless steel, smaller but in every other way identical to his Kikan. Now he felt cheated, as though he'd paid for an original painting and found it was a print. At the top of the hill the first thing he saw outside the apartment was the ambulance. He didn't make a connection until he saw the fitter being led away by two policemen, one of them carrying a shotgun. The fitter's eyes were bright with tears.

A Pearl's Tale

Carol McGuigan

And the city shall never try to be Barcelona,

or dress itself in luxury underwear.

Let it be salty, and rusty with iron,

keep secrets beneath its potent river.

Julia Darling

The ceiling is wedding cake white, thick with cherubs and gilt. A view of heaven, Janice thinks, as the carpet prickles her back. Her heels dig into the pile as Daniel looms over her, ready. The clocks make a coiling sound, like cobras, before they strike the hour.

Her interview is on a Wednesday afternoon. Inside the ticking honeycomb that is Cuthbertson's Jewellers, she sits on a straight-backed chair. The city noise seems dim. Let me fit in here, she pleads at the clocks that seem to fill every corner.

Mr Cuthbertson, hunched and black-suited, writes careful notes on her form. His gold pen hovers over her third last line of address.

"Battle Hill," he repeats.

Janice blushes; her one smart suit becomes tat.

"Yes." She reaches for her bag but he tells her she has the job. For a trial period.

She's to be trained by Daniel and the moment she sees him, she knows; he could craft her destiny. She has to stand by and watch him her whole first week. She's allowed to do little things, like make tea, which she takes to Mr Cuthbertson, trying not to rattle the cup. She watches Daniel with awe. With the grace of an aristocrat, he charms every customer so they leave adored and adorned. She's struck by his long, tanned hands and his different pair of cuff studs each day. Gold, white gold or jet. He must be on proper money, she thinks, as she starts to look for a flat.

In a role-play, Daniel shows her how to support a young lady's hand, in order to place the ring. Always young lady, never this lass or that wife. Janice wants to retrain her tongue. She practises when he asks her a question.

"Have you ever been engaged?"

"No." She says the word slowly but it's too stretched and ends up sounding like "now."

Daniel brings out another ring and her finger stretches towards it. He tilts her wrist so the gemstone glistens.

"Look at that lustre," he says.

He places her hand back on the velvet rest. She wants to ask if he's been engaged but curls in her fingers to hide her nails. From a white silk box Daniel produces a diamond solitaire. Her hand rises up, as if on a cloud. The icy bright stone is pure sanctuary.

Suddenly a dead weight thuds at the closed shop door. Hair, cement-dusty ginger, pokes over the gap in the blind. Janice wants to warn Daniel, as he crosses the carpet, not to open the door. She wants to flee up the staircase, hide in a grandfather clock, but she sits rigid as Daniel slides open the bolts.

"Where'sha?"

The edge of the counter digs into her back as Daniel lets Denny in. Scuffed boots stomp towards her, followed by Daniel's black shoes.

"Wassamarra ye nevah rang 'uz?"

Janice stares at the mobile gripped in his dusty white fist.

"This is Janice's training hour. If you could come back at…"

"Ah'm askin' arra question!"

Chandelier droplets quiver above Janice's head. She's mute.

"A'wuh gannin oot or wat?"

Janice takes a breath then offers back a neat, round word that doesn't rhyme too much with 'cow'. Her heart pounds under her smart lapels. Denny's mouth goes slack; he crinkles his Gregg's bag. He's only a labourer, Janice thinks. She used to call him a builder. At last, Daniel's arm arcs and guides Denny back to the door and Janice watches with quiet surprise as Denny shuffles out. But as Daniel locks the mortise, Denny's eye rears at the glass with one last desperate lunge.

"POOF!"

The door rattles, then is silent and Janice imagines her ex stamping off, mouth crammed full of pasty. She takes off the ring as Daniel returns to the counter. He carefully polishes it clear of smudges. Rubbing me away, Janice thinks. He turns his back, and Janice wants to scream, "I'm not like that! That's not who I am." But Denny's coarse blast hangs in the air like chip fat and her hope sinks into lard.

Daniel turns to face her, her legs are weak with shame. But held between each of his thumbs is a gossamer golden thread, suspending a pale moon droplet made of purest pearl. Janice gasps out loud. Daniel walks up behind her and gets in close, looping his arm past her face. She bows her head and lets his hot breath bathe her neck as he fastens the clasp. Janice's breastbone thuds.

"Would you like this?" he asks her.

Janice walks through the precinct that night, on the way home to her mam's. The pendant offers protection. She walks past aluminium shutters and lanky sports-clad lads, past the houses of the ones pushing thick-handled buggies while she's got a job in the town. She walks quickly past The Hind. A slur of karaoke blasts out behind her as someone opens the door.

"How man! Janice!"

She turns to see Denny steady himself on the door. His eyes swim in his head and a tight-vested girl with sleek dark hair makes a grab for his arm.

"Haway man back, Den, leave her, she's just a tight little snob."

Denny nods his sozzled head and waves his hand at Janice in a gesture she hopes means good riddance. She fills with a light excitement and walks up the grey paved path where the wind always whips at her hair. She squeaks open the gate and sees her mam and knows her life will be lifted from this and that the lifting started tonight.

But she doesn't show her mam her nice new necklace because she's not really sure if it's hers.

"See how it makes you feel," Daniel had said, "but keep it hidden from view."

It's a test, like the princess and the pea.

In her narrow bed, the pearl seems to pulse, like a tracking device. Tagged by Daniel, she'll soon fly this coop and find her true home – a city centre flat to start with. Apartment, she corrects herself out loud.

"You're a good team." Mr Cuthbertson smiles through watery eyes and tells Janice to come and see him.

She watches him walk away from the door of the tiny shop kitchen.

"He's half blind." Daniel whispers behind her, seeing her hand on the pearl.

She wants to ask Daniel if she can treat it as hers now or whether still to keep it hidden. Daniel's hand burns at her back as she makes Mr Cuthbertson's tea.

"Keep it close to your heart." He puts his finger to his lips.

Mr Cuthbertson's desk is at the head of the staircase in front of a pendulum clock.

"To purvey fine goods, one must know them intimately," he says, sipping the tea she's made. He reaches into his inside pocket and pulls out a slim leather box. Putting it down on the desk, he lifts out a glint of gold. Not a pen, but a knife.

"My wife," he says, holding it.

The top of the handle is tooled as the head of a woman. A shining, golden face.

"She was always with me." Mr Cuthbertson smiles tenderly. "It was modelled on her."

He replaces the knife in the box and closes the lid. It remains on the desk between them.

"She understood the conundrum of value." His voice has an edge to it. "I want you to stay under Daniel's tutelage."

Heat floods her arms.

"We'll extend your trial period."

She feels bewildered.

"You need further training."

She gets up wobbly. She'd hoped for a proper contract to fund an apartment's deposit. What can she still have to learn?

Next day, Janice shirks away from the poorer customers. Imitating Daniel, she proffers a seat to a well-heeled woman with Italian-looking glasses. The woman glares at her, sweeps round the shop once and leaves. Janice watches Daniel serve a tattooed couple. No chair offered there, just politeness and sale. She'll never be that good, he's instinctive. He and Mr Cuthbertson are somehow in league. She'll always be outside, a peasant skivvy good for nothing, she thinks as she washes the cups. She nods, head down, when Daniel tells her he'll be ten minutes late tonight. She looks up to see him gazing at her, in the mirror above the sink.

"Tonight you become the elite."

The chimes of the big outdoor clock hit six. Janice waits nervously in the lamp-lit glow. She fears she might fail this next test, that she's been kidding herself. Daniel arrives, his overcoat glistening. He shakes his big umbrella. She stands as he walks towards her.

"You'll need to wear this." He hands her a stiff white bag, embossed with a famous name. "Take your clothes off in there." He nods towards the little vestibule where Mr Cuthbertson does the accounts.

Speechless, Janice stumbles into the cramped little space and draws the thick dark curtain. She peers into the bag. A feather silk garment lies like a sleeping bird. She lifts up its weightlessness on thin white straps. When it falls around her shivering body, it feels invisible. The pearl seems to throb at her chest; she walks back into the shop.

Daniel lifts her arms to see how the fabric clings and leads her to the middle of the room. Already armed with jewelled clips, he fastens up her hair.

"It's important to become well acquainted with wealth if you haven't been born to it." He tells her to relax.

He circles her and clasps her neck with diamonds, binds platinum round her wrists, pins tiny sapphires in her ears and locks her ankle with silver. His eyes burn with pleasure as he raises a glittering tiara to place upon her head.

"No…" Janice starts.

He fixes the band at her crown.

Janice squirms at the idea of being so deserving, but Daniel gently leads her up the staircase to the full-length mirror and her bettered self. She looks – privileged, ascendant. From behind her, Daniel puts his hands on her hips, they linger, then move upwards, squeezing at her flesh. His mouth falls wet on her shoulder.

"Beautiful." Leaning into her, he guides her to the floor.

Janice's eyes flick over his shoulder, at Mr Cuthbertson's desk. The little box containing Mrs Cuthbertson is there, where he left it. She imagines the dead woman's fury as Daniel grunts and pushes inside her.

Later, when Janice emerges from the vestibule wearing her now drab-seeming suit, Daniel has tidied everything away and re-positioned the chairs. He's curt and businesslike as he bids her goodnight on the street.

These Monday nights continue for over a month and although Daniel is mostly silent, Janice senses his warmth. During the most recent, he breathed a passionate "thank you" into her neck. Like the pearl pendant, she knows to keep this a secret, until told otherwise. She's grown more self-assured. Her hands don't tremble when she handles real rubies or a Rolex watch.

But Sundays seem longer and longer. She flicks through a copy of *Status* and scans the photo pages. Well-coutured women seen at dances with bald, laughing men. TV sport comes up through the floor, her brother downstairs oblivious. She grips the window sill as the omnibus soap theme starts, grabs her jacket and runs.

The city centre feels hollow. Janice walks quickly to the exclusive development. Crossing the pavement, to the bright blue building, she thrills to its glassy edge. She squints up at a balcony and imagines watching a sunset or maybe jet-skiing friends. She walks around the sign boards, with the colourful blown-up photos – glamorous happy people living lives in London or New York. She shivers as a breeze gusts up. Pulling her jacket tighter she sees a man with a deep-fried complexion methodically searching the bins. He spots her and diagonally staggers over.

"Javenny sp'chinch daarlin'?"

His eyes are a lonely blue. Janice tries to move away but the man grasps her hand.

"I need ye to save uz pet."

She lurches at his desperation but prises his fingers from her wrist. His mouth twists to curse her but lets out a howl of despair. He hunches over, into himself, crying deep dry sobs. Janice swings away, into a whirlwind of grit. Sections of Sunday supplements fling themselves at her head. Screwing up her eyes, she pushes through the spinning pages of holidays and business news. She has to peel a sheet from her back. On it is Daniel upside down. Twisting the page around, she sees him in black tie, holding the hand of a pale young woman. She reads the caption three times.

'Wedding Bells for daughter of billionaire Bob' question mark.

A paragraph speculates whether Bob's daughter will be seen with her 'beau' at Monday night's Hunters' Ball.

Even before she gets to work, Janice is plotting. The clocks beat a pulse to her plan. She'll leave after work, she won't go home, she'll travel in what she's wearing.

She watches, in the late afternoon, Daniel leaving early, without a backward glance. Then Mr Cuthbertson says he's feeling unwell and asks if she minds locking up.

After everyone's gone, she sits alone with the blinds drawn, toying with the slim leather box. Mr Cuthbertson is more careless with his wife than he likes to crack on, leaving her all alone. Maybe all men did this. Once they got the lid on a woman, they discarded her. There's a glint in Mrs Cuthbertson's eye as Janice lifts up the knife. It slips in neatly with her pens, in her inside pocket, its cold fine edge at her breast.

Soon, Janice travels through the dark on the northbound 108. The only passenger, she sits on the empty top deck, rattling into the night. Her face looks gaunt in reflection.

She sniffs the country air as she watches the tail lights of the bus trundle away. Dark fields surround her. She can see The Lodge windows at the end of a long tarmac drive. Even from here, she can hear the sounds of a party. It starts to rain as she sets off, cold sleet soaking her clothes.

At last her shoes squelch into a warm room full of tinkling laughter and the smell of roasted lamb. Well made-up faces glance quickly at her mud-spattered tights and wild hair. She pushes through cummerbunds and taffeta. She shoulders her way to the dance floor and sees Daniel's gliding form. The lass from the newspaper is held in his arms. In her ears are the emeralds Janice wore last week, in her hair the tiara, and the solitaire on her left hand is on her pale third finger. A harsh male grip twists Janice's upper arm.

"Are you with the catering?" A tall man with blond nostril hair looks down at her.

Janice's face swings back to the dance floor but Daniel isn't there. From a taxi later, she watches all that colour, life and happiness recede, as she's driven back into shadow.

Later still, she stands naked in her room with only Mrs Cuthbertson for company. The snapped gold chain in one hand, the pearl drop in the other. She lifts the gold knife and traces it over her chest. Maybe it can only open letters, not the stupid heart of a girl who didn't know who she was. She looks at the face on the handle. 'Value the one precious thing you have,' it seems to be saying and Janice knows then, it isn't her heart she should cut.

The stall holders look at her curiously, still in her smart disguise. Half past eight on Tuesday morning, the hem of her skirt still damp but her suit pressed neat again. She's sat on a stool in the caff in the old covered market. Why's she here with the wrinkles and chiffon, coughs and broken hopes? But they don't know she's coming back, that they'll all know her name quite soon.

She sips her milky tea and watches a butcher boy cleave his way through a carcass. Dancing round the block like a boxer, he hammers and twists at the red flesh and bone, reducing it all to choice cuts. An older man handles a pile of glistening offal with cellophane gloves, arranging it on a white tray. Checking the knife in her pocket, Janice gets up to go.

The door of the shop is open, Mr Cuthbertson there already. His face looks five years younger. He greets her beamingly.

"This is Inspector Guardino."

A large man with a face like a brick stares back unsmiling. Two uniformed coppers pore over the cabinets like house flies. Janice's legs twitch.

"Daniel…" she begins.

Mr Cuthbertson raises his hand.

"It's all right my dear." He explains how everything has been caught on camera.

Every lusty Monday feast, dressed and served on the carpet. He continues, pointing out the lenses, cleverly hidden among the crowded clocks, round and glassy.

"I had them fitted once you started. Daniel didn't know, which is why he became so bold." He looks sad. "It used to be he only borrowed things. They'd be back the next day. It was worth it to keep him. But…" His voice trails off.

A young officer behind them discreetly closes the door, sealing them off from the city. Mr Cuthbertson looks at her sadly.

"You see Janice, Daniel thought gifts would win a rich girl's heart. Turn a shop boy into a prince." He shakes his head, eyes kind. "But we know, don't we? We brats from Battle Hill. This is the best we can hope for."

Janice feels a traitor inside the benevolent fortress. She hands over the key and the knife. Mr Cuthbertson unwinds the fine gold chain from the knife's handle and frees the dangling pearl. He hands it back to her.

"I'm sorry we had to use you as bait, this is yours as recompense."

A River's Tale

Daniel J Krupa

I cannot get to my love if I would die;

For the water of Tyne runs between her and me

And here I must stand with a tear in my 'ee,

Both sighing and sickly, my sweetheart to see.

Anonymous

"Toon Armeee! Toon Armee! Howay the lads!"

The words break into the cold air, slicing their way toward me. I hear them every other Saturday. I hear people say it, shout it, sing it, but never whisper it. And, just like every other Saturday, I'm walking my path, my solitary pilgrimage. It's a cold day: the wind hits me as I reach the bridge. Today is not the greatest of days, but it is one of the most beautiful; the sun is out, and shining a brilliant white, but I know there'll be a black cloud looming somewhere – somewhere the sun can't reach it and burn it away. The wind cuts my skin deep – forgot my scarf! Shit! Never mind: I'll make do, will do another button up and keep moving. My face and hands are used to it by now.

My chest is beginning to freeze, capillaries begin to hide and bury themselves, and I become pale. Cars rush past beside me, pulling the air with them, as I look out over the river; looking through gaps between green metal girders, feeling like a prisoner, but a prisoner with the greatest view. The sun is shining so clear today, I can't even look at it; the best I can do is look at its reflection in the river. The wind has provoked the river to become savage and restless, and consequently the imitated sun is less than exact. No longer a perfect orb: it is reflected but the waves continually tear it apart. You can still catch glimpses of the light, but only fragments, like an exploded jigsaw, tiny pieces here and there, fragments of brilliant light scattered upon the river.

I make myself stop looking at the river and continue on my way. Certainly, I no longer want to look to my right, but I know I will. I just have to look. Just like you have to see just how wet 'wet paint' really is, and like you have to look upon stained and mangled motorway metal, the same pervasive ethereal power took me now. I look and I see – just like I knew I'd have to, just like I knew I would. And there it is, not one of the great pieces of modern art I admit, but the best these lame hands could offer at the time: a heart, simple and true, framing two sets of initials. That was then, this is now, and the heart still resembles what was intended months ago, but the initials have lost their definition; the bottle green paint has been flaking, and falling away, as the wind gets underneath and tears it away to fly in the breeze. The initials could very well be someone else's, at least now they have no discernible skeleton, but I know those are mine, and those are yours, and the bridge shares our scars. I consider the melodrama of my lament, cringe, and walk on. I try not to think, but I can't help but think: I wonder when those initials began to fade? The first time you didn't come home? The first time I didn't pick up one of your calls with excitement? When lightning no longer pulsed through every blood vessel in this body when we were together? I don't know. I'll never know; I could spend eternity traipsing through our cemetery of memories, and pass forever wading in our decaying garden of valentine flowers, and still no answer would be promised, no sense of understanding guaranteed. I'll never know – never have, never will. Faded, gone, but the heart remains.

No more bridge left now, only city streets. One road dividing into many, and I wander down those that seem familiar, when everything else seems strange. The strangest feeling has taken control: I can see myself, I can see myself hurting but I cannot reach out to myself, and tell me there is nothing wrong and nothing to fear, that everything will be all right, will be okay. Maybe familiar streets are what I need. The comforting reassurance so often found in what is known so well. I could paint you these streets, right down to the flaws in the concrete, the different shades of grey concrete, and where every uneven square slab is to be found and avoided. But not today. Today they seem unfamiliar, strange, deceptive; I notice things I'm sure were never there before. Finally, I reach where I'm going to. I reach my salvation.

Walking through the doors, my chest begins to thaw. A cloud of whitish grey smoke floats around the room; it remains fixed, just above head height, the atmosphere of this inside world. Walking into the room, the smoke rushes toward me, filling my lungs, smothering my face, finding and forcing its way down my nose and throat reaching my lungs, this fiery air burns slightly. This is what my clothes and hair will smell like tomorrow – great! The smoke is silently swirling around the room, the opaque whispers of those that sit quietly at the bar, only breaking their silence to order another pint. Flickering bandit lights dance in endless repetition in the corner of my eye. People sit in groups, they sit side by side, they sit opposite each other, and they sit together. I hear their collective din of conversation, laughter, and song. It fills my ears until it's hard to hear myself let alone the man behind the bar asking me what drink I want, even though he's right in front of me. I ask for what I always ask for, continuing to search for solace in ritual. Doesn't work, it just doesn't taste right – might be off. Taking my drink from the bar, I see familiar faces but they don't see me. Shall I go sit with them? They haven't seen me so I don't have to, I'm not obliged to. Instead, I go and sit on my own, well just my drink and me, all alone in the non-smoking section; my clothes smell, my hair smells, but the drink is not beyond salvation.

No one else in this little cordoned off area, just me. People occasionally glance at me; they look at me like some animal in a zoo cage, or like a goldfish in a tank. I feel like they're going to come up and tap on the glass, make funny faces, and still act like they are the superior ones. I place my drink down, after taking another sip. I place it down, and wipe the condensation from my hand onto my jeans, streaking them a darker colour. Hundreds of grey overlapping broken circles adorn the table top – it's never been properly cleaned, maybe occasionally and fleetingly meeting a damp cloth, but only a brief and transient meeting – some look like horseshoes, others resemble tiny little alcoholic halos, others are simply perfect circles. I lift my glass up, time for another mouthful, and I leave my own little broken circle, making my own mark. Here I sit in my isolation of choice, just this disappearing drink and me. I sit alone, I drink alone and read the beer mat, which I'm not using but playing with.

Feeling quite self-conscious now; eyes rest heavy upon you when you're by yourself, with nobody to share the burden of a glance. I do the same thing every time I feel like this – every time I feel like every movement I make will be observed, extracted from context, analysed and, ultimately, ripped apart to expose my every defect, every failing and all my shortcomings as a person (a little paranoid, I admit) – I take my phone out from my inner jacket pocket. No text messages – great, and that's why I now always seem to equate the feeling of neglect with a blank phone screen and no longer a frozen Christmas puppy. I pretend to have one anyway. Fake the fact that someone broke away from their life, for maybe just two minutes, to write me something. I fake it pretty well, thumbing the keypad with what seems like guided intent when, in fact, my thumb is as lost as me. Sometimes, well most times, I can hide aimless wandering – I've made somewhat a life of it. Trying to look busy when there's nothing to do, trying to fit in, trying to disappear, be part of a crowd. If they can't see me, they can't hurt me. I begin to think again, and all this, all this which surrounds me, all these displeasing dissonant sounds, all of their glances, instantly seem somewhat less important. My thoughts belong to me, they will never know what I hold inside.

I no longer love her, that's for sure, but maybe I love her. Sometimes, in quiet moments, quiet moments like these, I think to myself; and in these times I make my memories play with me. I look for the shadowy illusions of life that hide within me, seeking them out in the recesses of my mind; taking them, I breathe colour and life into them, I make them move and I make them real – my Frankenstein memories, I give them life. I know I cannot let the past die, it is my flaw: continually, I resurrect what I have lost, and, endlessly, I relive what is past, kicking myself in the stomach for every mistake I made, for every time I was less than I could have been. Sometimes, just sometimes, they seem so real. And occasionally, but only occasionally, it's like nothing changed, nothing went wrong, and everything is still in its right place, including me. But I cannot live in dreams made of cobwebs. The past offers nothing new.

My eyes begin to search new parts of the room. They move away from the confines of the phone, the beer mat, my shoes – what is that on the bottom of my shoe? Don't want to know. The sun is still shining outside, and now is beginning to break into the room. Penetrating shafts of light, with their strong, sharp, golden edges, slice the room; dark from light becomes divided, the light making the dark darker, and itself more pure. Constantly, they stream into the room; they have no beginning, no end, just an infinite middle bleaching gold. It pours through, unrestrained, burning every shadow in touches. Dark and light, black and white, side by side, I see before me. I look up to the window but I'm made to close my eyes by what I see. Behind the safety of my eyelids I can sort of see what I tried to look at, sunbeams have delicately burned the shape of the window frame into my exposed retina. It will heal. It will fade in time.

My eyes open. My eyes readjust, and I look closer. Now I'm no longer looking through the light, seeing the drinkers, the football supporters, the old man with his pint of Guinness; instead I'm looking directly into it. There, right between the defining lines of light that dissect this room, I can see a million tiny dust particles effortlessly dancing before me. They rise and fall together, tumble and glide in perfect time, never colliding, the air always keeping them apart. The light hits them, bouncing off each individual speck, making it seem as though a little tiny universe exists there before me, for me. My own little galaxy of stars dances just for me.

Beyond this, I see the faces I've seen every week for, well, forever; ever since I was the height of my father's knee I've known these faces. Ever since I first wore the black and white. Ever since then, I've never sat alone. Sliding back my seat, I move away from my isolation in the non-smoking section, move away from my segregation from those for whom there is no division, from those for whom there never could be a divide. Moving through the beam of light, for the briefest moments I pause – it even begins to burn me, not with rosy warm fingertips but with fiery fingers that dig and carve rashes into my skin, but I do have the palest skin, as pale as a Scandinavian albino; I assure you, I could even make a ghost look ethnic. As I wait my skin begins to react, I can feel the cells tingling, I can feel them on fire, but I am only there for the most brief and transient of moments. I think. I know that this stupor, this desolate world of self-pity and self-loathing I have condemned myself to, is all my making, is all my fault, it is pathetic. I am alone because, simply, I choose to be. I think all of this in my brief moment in the sun.

Moving out of this shadowy corner, I take my rightful place by those I feel no separation from. Today we wear the same, speak the same, feel the same. If I hurt right now, I know the person next to me will know my pain before I truly do; and they will be right there beside me when I jump in elation. It is here, with my people, my friends, I realise my colours run deep. They always have, even on a day like today, which is not the most beautiful of days. I know everything will be okay because no matter how much I choose to be alone, I know I never will be.

The bells ring, words are shouted, closing time comes. As if the final day had come, silence descends, and men prepare to be judged by loved ones upon returning home. Silence has a funny effect upon time, it somehow is able to warp and stretch a second; a moment spent with a laugh hanging in the air passes so fleetingly, its nature so transient, but the very same moment spent with silence seems to extend for a thousand eons. This is one of those moments where silence reigns. Cigarettes begin to die in full ashtrays, releasing their final carcinogenic cough; their final whisper is spoken to the room, for tonight anyway. I look around at the tables, and the remains of the day. What seems like hundreds of glasses cover the top of the bar, mainly pint glasses, some half pints, and some smaller tumblers. On the tables brown ale, from broken shards, flows in careering rivulets, following the guiding grain of the wood, until it tumbles over the edge.

Closing time, and I'm injected back into the world, to amble down these streets with less than balletic grace. I hear singing somewhere, echoing down back alleys and bouncing off buildings, the songs of victory find their way to me. It seems silly and ludicrous that your weekly happiness is dependent on eleven men and a ball, but that is only to those who don't understand.

I walk home in the dark, retracing my steps. I'm taken back over the bridge. I stop in the same place as I did this morning to observe the sun. No sun, only moon. And it is here, among the tremulous shadows of the night, which tangle and coil around me, that I think about you. The lights from cars make these shadows constrict, and I think about you more. I look down into the river, and I wonder just how hard this river would be; certainly, it's black enough to be hard as volcanic glass, I wonder if it's as hard. The river is completely black now; completely black, except for the second moon, the reflected moon, and the glistening varnish of phosphorous moonbeams that bounce off the surface. The river is so much calmer than it was this morning. No sun now, only moon. I stand, leaning on the bridge, and looking upon this object in the sky, as naively as a child looking up to the mobile that hangs above its crib. The moon, the sun's mirror, this perfect white circle, is rendered so precisely upon the river. The river is no longer so tumultuous. Now, ripples only momentarily distort the image, before returning it to its original perfection. I often wonder where the sky ends and the ground begins during my days, but during my nights they always seem one and the same; and looking upon this river and looking upon this sky, never have I ever been surer that there is no division, no divide.

The silence is broken by the muffled melody coming from my jacket – a text message. I take one last look: the black Tyne and the perfect white circle, the black and the white, and I walk away.

The Runner's Tale

David Darton

It's wrong to think that every race has only one winner. Running is about improving yourself, and if you run faster... than the last time then you're a winner.

Brendan Foster

"Daddy is the champion, Daddy is the champion," Andrew chanted, before launching himself at his father with all the might a six-year-old could muster.

Brian staggered back as he caught his son. How much longer, he wondered, would he be able to swing Andrew around like this? He choked back tears that seemed to come unbidden all the time at the moment.

"Come on, we'd better get you ready. Mummy will be here soon."

Right on cue, the buzzer went. Brian pressed the button that released the gate at the bottom of the stairwell. The new gate made a difference. Jarrow, the source of the famous workers' march in the 1920s depression, should have more pride about it. But parts, like this estate, suffered just the same as ever. The difference between here and the Newcastle Quayside, where he and Sarah had lived in their trendy flat, was larger than ever.

For once Sarah did not seem to know quite what to say. Andrew ran to her. "Mummy, Daddy's going to be in another race," he told her excitedly.

"So, you're still going to do the Great North Run?"

Brian nodded. One of their many awkward silences began to develop as Andrew chatted to himself while his mother helped him into his coat. Brian knew that Sarah wanted to disapprove of his plan to run, but couldn't quite bring herself to.

"I *am* sorry, you know," she said finally.

Brian nodded.

"But it doesn't make any difference," she continued.

"No," Brian said flatly. Nothing ever would.

"Come on, Andrew. We have to go." Turning to Brian. "We'll talk."

"Yes."

Andrew ran to his father and tried to high-five him. But he

hadn't quite got the hang of it, so just hugged him around the waist. Brian stroked his hair.

"Come on, we have to go. Don't worry to come down, Brian."

The door closed. The tears came.

Tom settled back in his first class seat as the Mallard 225 pulled smoothly out of King's Cross for the three-hour train journey to Newcastle. He was the only one in the compartment reserved for first class ticket holders at the weekend.

He was used to being the only one. The only black kid in his public school. The only black barrister in the chambers. He became more, not less, conscious of his colour as he got older and reached levels of society where his colour was increasingly rare. And the depressing part of it was that the new generation of black children were still failing to climb the greasy pole as readily as their white counterparts.

Tom stretched out his six foot three frame and flirted remorselessly with the sparky Newcastle lass who served him coffee from the trolley. He knew he looked really good, his body toned from all the training he had been doing for the Great North Run, and muscles rippling from his thrice-weekly workout in the gym.

The biggest half-marathon in the world. More than fifty-thousand people running, most for charity. The organisers promised that the 2005 run would be even more of a spectacle and celebration than in previous years. But none of that was the point. This time he was going to beat not only his personal best, but all the other forty entrants from his running club too. Especially that upstart Ellis. They all went on about how the important thing was to improve on your own personal best. That you weren't competing with each other. But that was shit. He had had to compete all his life. Running was the physical competition that paralleled the mental striving of his work life. And he was not going to lose. He never lost.

The sun was sinking as they came into Newcastle. The train stopped on the bridge awaiting a platform. Tom looked down to the river hundreds of feet below, the steep banks aglow with lights in the dusk and the new Millennium Bridge with its spectacular arch just visible. It looked like a sophisticated metropolis of the future. If you squinted a bit.

Central Station was confusing, but Tom eventually found his way out and followed the directions down the steep path to the Copthorne Hotel on the river bank below, his sports bag slung easily over his shoulder.

Brian was always restless before a big run. At least, though, he would cook properly for himself for once. He had to stock up on the slow-release carbs that pasta would provide, and he actually enjoyed making the sauce.

This year, he was even more unsettled than usual. First, there had been the news crew. Turning up at his door unexpectedly. He wondered who had told them. He realised that he was a minor local celebrity, having taken part in every Great North Run since its inception and one memorable year coming close to the time of the elite runners. But he knew he was no elite runner. Basically a middle-of-the-packer who, at one point of peak fitness, had had a particularly good race. But now, of course, he was *real* human interest news. All the ingredients for the 'soft spot' at the end of the local news bulletin.

And then there was the call from Sarah. She had sounded softer, even kind. The first sign of a thaw since she had discovered his stupid affair. An affair that, if he was honest, *had* meant a lot to him. But then had suddenly meant *nothing* to him when Sarah found out. He knew that he and Sarah were meant to be for life. But the hurt had been too much, and finally the split was a relief to both of them. The feelings, though, were still there. He knew they were.

But of no use now. Not enough time to rebuild.

Tom had stayed in many anonymous four-star hotel rooms. But somehow this one felt worse. Probably because he knew there was nothing in his life to really look forward to at the moment. His life was as sterile as the room he was in, luxurious but empty. No one to share it with and no aim other than to strive.

He flicked on the television. The regional news bulletin was starting. He hated provincial, insignificant, twiddle twaddle and was about to turn it off when the newscaster turned to the Great North Run.

"There is a record number of confirmed entrants in this year's run, that will have even more bands than usual to create the traditional carnival atmosphere." The screen showed scenes from last year's run. "Six hundred and thirty thousand runners have crossed the line in the twenty-four years of the race, but only very few runners have competed every year, among them our own Brian Vinton, who first ran it when he was fifteen. Tragically, this is likely to be Brian's last race, and is a particular act of courage among so many who push themselves to the limit for good causes."

The shot changed to a picture of a man in a bright scarlet running vest. The voice-over continued.

"Brian was diagnosed last month with an inoperable cancer and expects to live for only a few more months. He is determined to do the Great North one final time, and has sponsorship totalling nearly two and a half thousand pounds for Leukaemia Research. I asked Brian earlier today how he felt about tomorrow, especially as his cancer is weakening his heart and doctors have told him that it could be dangerous to over exert himself."

"Well, Donald, I have thought about this a lot and…"

Tom switched the set off angrily. He hated the way that people displayed weakness for sympathy and support. So the guy was going to die. We were all going to die. He had never made anything of his disadvantages to get special treatment. Anyway, he didn't want to be distracted. He wanted to focus on beating Ellis and being number one in his club.

Crowds were swarming out of Haymarket Metro station and a long trail of people streamed across the pedestrian crossing in brightly coloured vests and shorts – and in various animal and character fancy dress costumes. Brian could sense one or two people pointing him out, and a few came and shook his hand and wished him good luck. A couple with southern accents in front of Brian were commenting on the wonder of the Metro trains with no drivers. Brian remembered how fascinated he used to be with this when the system first opened.

He usually had a mix of emotional feelings as he approached the valley that cut through the park and saw it overflowing with thousands of runners. But everything was heightened this time. He supposed that without the possibility of death nothing would be sharp and meaningful in life.

This morning had been hard. Sarah had agreed to take Andrew to see him near the finishing line, on the last flat stretch of the course that ran along the coast at South Shields. But she had turned up unexpectedly at the flat this morning with Andrew so that they could walk together to the Metro. Andrew seemed to sense that there was something momentous in the occasion and had been unusually quiet, just holding his dad's hand firmly and not saying much. Brian looked down at his son. Should he be taking the risk? Taking the risk that they would lose out on a few more months of memories? But he had been through this time and time again in his mind. He couldn't go out on a whimper. He had a short time left and wanted his son to remember him as strong, not just as the weedy wimp he was sure to become as the illness took hold.

At the entrance to the Metro Sarah had taken his hand. The first time she had touched him since he moved out. She squeezed it and gave him a thin envelope.

"Read it when you finish the run. Andrew and I will be waiting at the same place we waited two years ago." Then she unclasped Andrew's hand from his, lifted him up to kiss his dad good luck, and turned, walking briskly away towards the car.

Even Tom felt a moment of awe, of being involved with his fellow man in something bigger than himself. He stood on one of the bridges across the valley and looked at the tens of thousands now gathered. A famous sports commentator's voice was echoing through the speakers, whipping up periodic enthusiastic cheers. This was interspersed with uptempo music. Helicopters were whirring overhead. Tom made his way down the bank, walked up past the enclosure for the elite runners and finally pushed himself through into the crowd of expectant runners, manoeuvring himself forward towards the front, close to the foremost sign for runners expecting to do the course in less than one hour thirty minutes. He knew from the TV pictures last night that it was important to be as far forward as possible if the worst of running through thousands of flaying arms and legs was to be avoided.

Oh God. There was that man from the television. The one with cancer in the bright scarlet vest. Tom couldn't think of his name. Surely he couldn't run this fast? Look at all those people fawning over him. But Tom couldn't quite keep it up. There was something infectious about the atmosphere. And he supposed the Cancer Man was braver than most. There *was* something defiant about doing this in the face of death that Tom could relate to.

He began his warm-up routine and started to feel more relaxed until… "Tom! How you feeling? Looking forward to it?"

Ellis. In all these thousands how could he have ended up in the same spot? As if reading his mind, Ellis continued in his public school, Oxbridge vowels, "Saw your head above all the others and forced my way down here. It's your first Great North, isn't it? Just save a bit for the long hill at eleven miles, just before we drop down to the coast for the last stretch. What time you hoping for?"

"Nothing in mind really," Tom lied. "With all these people, high speeds are going to be difficult."

"Oh, it's not too bad if you are up front like we are here and can keep up the pace. I want to beat my last year's time – one hour twenty-four. My best ever half-marathon time, you know, despite the hills. I guess the bands and the cheering push you on harder than you'd otherwise do."

The gun went off for the start of the wheelchair race. Only a few minutes and the main race would be off. Brian couldn't relax. There was a tightness across his chest after this morning that he couldn't shift. He wondered if he should read the note that Sarah had given him. But he had promised not to look at it until afterwards. Surely he could be true to her this once?

Tom cleared the worst of the crowded field of runners as he came up the slope after the first underpass. He had done about a mile and was feeling good. He felt light, with long easy strides. The training was paying off. Alongside him was Ellis, but Tom sensed that he was finding it just a touch harder to keep up this initial pace than Tom was. If he could encourage Ellis to go slightly faster, he was sure he would then burn out. Tom would love the sense of flying past Ellis in the last mile or so.

Brian knew he was pushing himself too hard. The tightness he had put down to the emotional strain of the morning was still there. He had promised himself that he would not take an unnecessary risk; that he would keep below the maximum he was capable of, but somehow the push of such a large number of runners, the familiarity of the course and the cheering made it difficult to discipline himself. He wanted to do well. Just this one more time.

At four miles they had gone up the first long, but fairly gentle slope. He glanced over his shoulder. There was a tall black man who stood out from the others and who was running just slightly slower than him – about two hundred yards back. Brian would slow and let him overtake and then stay just behind him, knowing that if he did, he would be running just below his own capacity and would be much safer.

Tom had been concentrating on Ellis more than the other runners. He had goaded him a bit by saying what a pleasant, easy run this was and Ellis had taken the bait. Tom let him get a little way ahead and then sat on his tail about a hundred yards back, knowing he had the reserve strength to take him at any time. The five-mile marker came up. Tom checked his expensive running watch. Dead on his race plan time. As he looked up again he saw that he was passing the cancer man in his scarlet vest. The cheering was clearly not for Tom.

Eleven miles. The long hill up before the steep swing left down to the last mile along the coast. Brian felt better after a quick slug of water handed to him by a smiling lady at the water station. He had been right to let the black man pace him. But as the hill went on, the black man ahead seemed to slow. Brian steadily gained on him and felt it was now safe to pass him about half a mile short of the brow of the hill. There were dozens of runners around, but it was not the mad pack that he saw a mile back down the hill when he looked round.

Ellis was beginning to burn out as Tom had predicted. As they climbed the hill, he was slowing. Tom debated taking him then. But he decided to slow and maintain the hundred yards or so between them. He wanted the pleasure of really streaking past him on the home straight. The cancer man overtook him. No matter. Indeed he found himself yelling "Well done, go for it mate!" His only concern was Ellis.

Brian came up over the brow of the hill, anticipating the joy he always felt at this point as the sea came into view. It didn't fail him. The exhilaration seemed even more intense than in previous years as he swept down the steep hill to the coast. His head was pounding and he felt a tight pain in his chest, but somehow felt just great. He persuaded himself it was just the usual runner's high as the body flooded itself with endorphins.

Tom made his move on Ellis as they swept down the hill. But as he moved neck and neck with him, he realised that he had misjudged it a bit. Ellis had more in him than Tom expected, and they matched each other for a short while pace for pace on opposite sides of the wide, closed-to-traffic road. Then finally Tom began to pull away. He was going to do it. Ellis was now a few paces behind. Tom was flying, barely aware of the bands, the cheering and the other runners. Ahead he saw the scarlet vest of the cancer man. He was going to have to pass him to stay ahead of Ellis.

Suddenly the cancer man was falling to his side, collapsing onto the road in front of Tom. Oh shit no. "Out of my way!" He slowed his pace and jumped right over the cancer man, sprawled across the tarmac, aware of Ellis catching up to his right.

Tom screeched to a halt and Ellis flew past him. Jesus, what had he become? He turned back. Two runners had stopped. The usual scrawny runners standing ineffectually over the fallen man. Tom took a couple of strides back and leant over him. The man was gasping something. Tom leaned down.

"Don't let me go out in a whimper," he said, grasping desperately at Tom's vest. Tom thought he understood. No one else could lift him, but Tom could. He lifted him horizontally and put him across his shoulders. Jesus. He wasn't sure the man was still breathing. Tom looked up. Ellis was just crossing the finishing line a few hundred yards in front. Brian, that was his name, he suddenly remembered. He adjusted the weight of Brian across his shoulders, gradually becoming aware that the crowds nearby had gone completely quiet.

The bandleader saw what was happening. The band stopped what it was playing and struck up the tune from that film, *Officer and a Gentleman*, where the man picks up his girl and carries her out of her humdrum life to a better place. The crowd took it up:

Love lift us up where we belong,

Tom began jogging slowly towards the finish, steadying Brian on his shoulders.

Where the eagles cry on a mountain high.

The voices of the crowd swelled.

Love lift us up where we belong,

Tom lifted Brian almost above his head. Runners all around slowed and ran alongside.

Up from the world we know, where the fair wind blows.

Tom felt his eyes prickle. "You're not going out on a whimper," he whispered. Tears streamed down his face for the first time in years.

In the crowd, Andrew, sitting on his mother's shoulders, shouted excitedly, "Look at Daddy! Daddy is the champion, Daddy is the champion! Look, Mummy, they're lifting Daddy up like they always lift up champions. Daddy is the champion!"

Sarah felt numb. Somehow, she just knew he was dead. All she could think was whether he had read her short note before he died. *Come home. We'll work something out.*

Editor's Notes

Tyneside Tales follows on from the success of the York Tales, published in 2004. Inspired by the Canterbury Tales, each of the short stories in that collection was introduced by a quote from Chaucer. Inspired by the York Tales, each of the short stories in this anthology is introduced either by a quote from a person with a clear relationship with the area or a reference to a piece of writing which sparked off the idea for the story. These quotes add an extra layer to each tale by reaffirming the bond the anthology has with Tyneside. Again, as with the York Tales, the authors were also given explicit parameters in which to work. Each story was not only to reflect the physicality of Tyneside and capture the essence of the people who live and work there, but also the subject or theme of each Tale was to reveal an aspect of life here and now.

When choosing the stories for inclusion in the collection, I was therefore looking for tales which would not only captivate and enthral, but which would, when viewed as a whole, be connected and contrasted – in the same sense that contrasting individuals connect to create a society. Each narrative had to be unique; its idiosyncrasies sketching a scene that would be both revealing and engaging. Tyneside Tales forms a literary landscape where each view is different; whichever way you turn you'll find a distinct voice.

The variety of focus and tone, settings and themes to be found in this volume is testimony to the talent to be found in Tyneside. The stories range from challenging and provocative to poignant and humorous. Some of the tales feature characters that are instantly familiar; some open a peephole into other people's markedly unfamiliar lives. The subjects alternate between the momentous and the incidental, yet each narrative provides a true snapshot of contemporary life. Every short story in this collection is a social observation; each is thought provoking, insightful and instantly absorbing.

Although this collection of short stories is the result of a competition, it has been decided not to name the winning entries. It is not our intention to devalue the competition or the stories to which prizes were awarded, but rather to recognise the merit and diverse qualities of *all* the tales chosen for inclusion. I hope you enjoy reading them as much as I've enjoyed working with the authors who wrote them.

Rachel Hazelwood

Acknowledgements

We are delighted to acknowledge below the many people and organisations who released permission to quote their work to the **TALES series'** writers and to us.

It was indeed a long labour to track down the many contributors who have been used to open the stories. In some cases, it was not possible to find the source of our preferred quotes and, in rare cases, we were unable to obtain permission. Our writers, who are undeniably creative, have, in a few instances, been flexible enough to either change their preferred quote or even, on occasion, quote themselves!

The copyright laws are complex and fraught with danger for a small house like END*papers*, and we have made every effort to comply with the legislation as advised. We are deeply appreciative to each of the contributors listed below.

The Geordie Indieboy's Tale by James Darton

In trouble to be troubled

Is to have your trouble doubled

Taken from the writings of Daniel Defoe,
who spent a great deal of time in Newcastle, including as
a government agent, at the beginning of the 18th century

A Brother's Tale by Matt Charnock

We all do things like this; we have a stone that we
keep in our pocket which is a guarantee of life's
continuity, and it has to do with hoping that
things will all work out, that life will be okay.
Antony Gormley, an artist from Tyneside

The Tale of Micka's Christmas by Frances Kay

keep your feet still, Geordie hinny,
lets be happy through the neet
For we may not be so happy through the day;
So give us that bit of comfort,
keep your feet still, Geordie lad,
And divvent drive me bonny dreams away.
George Ridley

The Merchant's Tale by David Darton

I am seen where I am not,
I am heard where eyes is not,
Tell me now what I am,
and see that you misse me not
A riddle on the steeple of
St Nicholas's Church, Newcastle

The Motorist's Tale by Astrid Hymers

Whisht lads haad yor gobs
an aal tell yer an aaful story
(Listen lads, keep quiet,
while I tell you an awful story)
'Lambton Worm', a traditional
Northumbrian folktale and story

A Tale of Memory; the Tail of Love by Michael Pattison

Plants, parks and gardens never stop
changing, by day, by season or by year.
We have restored the park, but now we have
to let it grow. The next few years are
going to be exciting and challenging.
Adam Greenwold (Leazes Park Manager)

148

Natalya's Tale by Carol McGuigan

...we have no control over our place of birth,
but we live with the consequences forever.

Alan Plater
From 'Geordies'
edited by Robert Colls and Bill Lancaster,
Chapter Four, 'The Drama of The North East', page 71.
Published by Edinburgh University Press, 1992

Faith's Tale by Rachael Forsyth

Well the first time I saw her,
well I thought I didn't know her,
but I'm sure I'd seen her face before,
I couldn't think of where,
her blue eyes met mine in passing,
up the High Street in the morning,
and her look was so entrancing,
that me heart was mine nee mair.

'The Bonny Gateshead Lass', a traditional Tyneside folksong

The Homeleaver's Tale by Matt Forrester-Shaw

The best of men cannot suspend their fate.

Taken from the writings of Daniel Defoe,
who spent a great deal of time in Newcastle, including as a
government agent, at the beginning of the 18th century

An Angel's Tale by Dorothy Milne
Dance te yer Daddy, maa bonny laddy
Dance te yer Daddy, te yer Mammy sing
Ye shall have a fishy, on a little dishy
Ye shall have a fishy
When the boat comes in.
William Watson,
'Dance to yer Daddy' was originally printed in
'Allan's Tyneside Songs', 1862

A Tall Tale by Peter Marshall
Like someone's love once dreamed about
But not possessed and longed for now
'The Disappointment' by Sean O'Brien
(Collected in 'Cousin Coat')
Macmillan, London, UK

A Fashionable Tale by James Macfarlane
What happens in the Koan Interview is private
and must never be repeated.
James Macfarlane
Kikan is wordless, a koan response favoured by the
Rinzai sect who developed the Wabi style asceticism
influencing contemporary minimalist design.

A Pearl's Tale by Carol McGuigan

And the city shall never try to be Barcelona,
or dress itself in luxury underwear.
Let it be salty, and rusty with iron,
keep secrets beneath its potent river.

Taken from Julia Darling's poem
'A Short Manifesto for My City',
published in 'Apology for Absence',
Arc Publications, 2004 and reproduced here
by kind permission of Arc and Julia Darling's family

A River's Tale by Daniel J Krupa

I cannot get to my love if I would die;
For the water of Tyne runs between her and me
And here I must stand with a tear in my 'ee,
Both sighing and sickly, my sweetheart to see.

Taken from 'Waters of Tyne', anonymous,
first published in 1793

The Runner's Tale by David Darton

It's wrong to think that every race has only one
winner. Running is about improving yourself,
and if you run faster…than the last time then
you're a winner.

Brendan Foster, founder of the Great North Run

Author Biographies
(in alphabetical order)

Matt Charnock

Matt Charnock lives in York and works as a photographer. He enjoys coffee and cheesecake – but a coffee flavoured cheesecake he had once was rancid. Matt moved to York after graduating from Ripon and York St John College, where he studied Drama. Matt also tries to play squash.

David Darton

David is part-time strategy and research director of the Equal Opportunities Commission, a freelance business consultant, media trainer and writer. He has had several short stories and an illustrated children's story published. He has also written/edited a number of non-fiction titles. David has lived and worked in many parts of the country. He currently lives with his partner, Colin, and shares care of his three children.

James Darton

James Darton was born in 1987 and, through some outrageous displays of bluffing, cheating and begging, has survived long enough to be doing A level History, Film Studies, Philosophy and English at York College. He doesn't often write anything beyond the occasional text message; however he enjoyed writing 'Geordie Indieboy' and plans to write more in the future.

Matt Forrester-Shaw

Matt was born in 1973 for legal purposes and 1978 for anyone else who asks. He grew up in South East Essex, but eventually Matt flew the coop to London. There he enjoyed many nights of dancing and waking up in various locations with the words "Where's the station?" Matt then moved around the country and finally settled in Manchester.

Rachael Forsyth

After recently graduating with a BA in Music from Middlesex University Rachael is now teaching music to students around London. An avid player of the saxophone Rachael plays gigs with her band 'Soul Jam' and is looking to excel in the music world. She has been writing since she was at school and was fortunate enough to have an entry published in the 2004 *York Tales* anthology. She is now working on her second novel and is hopeful to see more of her work published in the near future.

Astrid Hymers

Married with three grown-up children, Astrid is an active member of Cullercoats Writers' Group. She's had several short stories published in local and national anthologies. In 2001 she was shortlisted in the category, 'Most Promising Unpublished Novel' in the National Association of Writers' Groups competition. Her monologue received 'Highly Commended' in 2004 and this year she is shortlisted in two categories: Best Short Story and Best Children's Short Story.

Frances Kay

Frances Kay began working in Newcastle upon Tyne in 1973 as a performer, writer and director with MAD BONGO THEATRE GROUP, which toured schools, prisons, pubs, theatres and communities in and around Tyneside for five years. In the eighties she was the Geordie puppet 'Cosmo' in BBC TV's preschool programme, *You and Me*. She now lives and works in Ireland and is currently writing children's plays for Team Theatre Company, Dublin.

Daniel J Krupa

Daniel J Krupa was born in 1986 in Blackburn, Lancashire. Daniel is currently studying English at the University of Durham. Amongst his favourite writers are Joseph Conrad and F. Scott Fitzgerald. Outside of literature his interests include film studies, particularly the work of Stanley Kubrick, Alfred Hitchcock, and Steven Spielberg. Daniel would one day like to be the author of several novels, or the director of several films.

Carol McGuigan

Carol McGuigan studied Film and Drama at Reading University and became an actress in the mid 1980s. Her first play was broadcast on Radio 4 and performed in the Assembly Rooms at the Edinburgh Festival in 1996. Since then, she has written mostly drama, with six more plays for the BBC and a handful for local theatre. Last year, her short story 'Agnostic', was published in *Mslexia*. She continues to act – see her as the librarian in the film Billy Elliot!

James Macfarlane

James Macfarlane began writing while working as an electrician in the Gorbals redevelopment and Clydeside shipyards. His fiction is driven by themes of cultural conflict and the paradox of development. He has written on classical and flamenco music, contributing reviews and features to *Classical Guitar*. He is studying Creative Writing at the University of Newcastle and lives with his wife and son overlooking the mouth of the Tyne.

Peter Marshall

Peter lives in York with his fiancée and is a hairy man. This is his first attempt to write a short story, or any story, come to think about it. Unless of course you count the one he wrote when he was six about the 'slime goons' and 'scuzz monsters'. He also writes and performs comic poetry around the city to great acclaim. He may one day write something serious.

Dorothy Milne

Dorothy Milne was born and still resides in the Tyneside area. She spends her time writing, travelling and gardening. Her inspiration and creativity for writing comes from everyday and often quite mundane situations. Her motivation stems from a very encouraging and supportive family, true friends and her two rescued cats which she adores. For the anthology, she chose to write about the Angel of the North because ever since its arrival on Tyneside it has held a mystical fascination for her.

Michael Pattison

At the time of writing, Michael is seventeen years old. He lives in Gateshead with his parents and older sister. Currently trapped in the murky abyss of education, he is studying A levels in Art, English, History and Media Studies. He is passionate about cinema, and hopes to become an artist through that medium, an ambition which is at once vague and precise.

About the TALES series

If you are interested in how a **TALES** anthology might be launched in your area then by all means contact us at *info@endpapers.co.uk* and of course be sure to check out the other titles in the **TALES series** and look out for forthcoming volumes on *www.endpapers.co.uk*

We launch short story competitions as a catalyst for local writers. We use the competition as a means to attract writers' attention to the very real possibility that their work might be published to wide acclaim within one year.

The **TALES series** represents a commitment to new writers and to 'villagisation' as opposed to 'globalisation'. We are all probably grateful for the smaller world we can now travel through more easily and more cheaply. Many of us doubtless enjoy the benefits of wider and wider availability of everything. What the **TALES series** has shown us, however, is that there is nothing quite like the local story, with a familiar backdrop, to engage our interest.

In 2004 we published **YORK TALES** which acted as our prototype.

In 2005 we have **BRISTOL TALES, GLASGOW TALES** and **TYNESIDE TALES**.

In 2006 **SHEFFIELD TALES** is already committed and we are in the process of selecting other areas in Northern Europe for this third batch.

There is no end to the creativity of story telling and the joys it can bring writer and reader and indeed publisher. We look forward to working with new writers across the world for years to come.

Magdalena Chávez
Creator of the **TALES series**

Book Club Notes

Book Club Notes

Book Club Notes

Book Club Notes